Contents

Challenge and Response

Critiques of the Catholic Bishops' Draft Letter on the U.S. Economy

Catholic Lay Commission • Peter L. Berger
Michael Novak • Robert J. Samuelson
Andrew M. Greeley • George F. Will
Charles Krauthammer • Philip F. Lawler

Appendix by Archbishop John J. O'Connor
Edited by Robert Royal

Ethics and Public Policy Center • Washington, D.C.

Foreword

THE U.S. CATHOLIC BISHOPS were embroiled in controversy over the first draft of their pastoral letter "Catholic Social Teaching and the U.S. Economy" even before its publication on November 11, 1984. Given the economic problems facing America and the diverse solutions being offered, it probably could not have been otherwise. The drafting committee of five bishops, headed by Archbishop of Milwaukee Rembert Weakland, decided not to issue the letter until after the presidential election so that it would not be viewed as a political statement. To judge by the response, this tactic failed.

Asserting that the distribution of income and wealth in the United States failed to meet even "minimal standards of distributive justice," the bishops endorsed or seemed to endorse several specific and highly controversial proposals, among them:

—large increases in domestic welfare programs and a substantial rise in the minimum wage;

—a national jobs program that would include "direct public service employment";

—a substantially greater federal role in coordinating and planning the U.S. economy;

—a "fundamental restructuring" of U.S. trade and foreign aid policies in ways similar to the proposals for a New International Economic Order.

The letter met with widespread criticism both inside and outside the Catholic Church. Many Catholics objected, not only to specific recommendations, but also to the bishops' use of their moral authority to support policies about which reasonable and committed Catholics sincerely disagree. Several Protestant critics made similar points. Secular critics generally pointed out that the bishops were calling for a greater commitment to policies that in the last two decades have not worked and have often had negative consequences.

To understand the bishops' larger intentions, it is helpful to know how they decided to write the pastoral on economics. Four years earlier, in November 1980, the bishops issued a pastoral letter on Marxist Communism that focused primarily on the contradictions between Marxist ideology and Catholic doctrine. It also strongly criticized Marxist states for their violations of human rights. Nevertheless, it counseled North Americans to cooperate when possible with Marxist regimes for "maintenance of world peace and eradication of global poverty." In light of this recommendation the bishops voted to write two additional pastorals: one on war and peace, and one on capitalism.

The pastoral on war and peace, which focused on nuclear arms (*The Challenge of Peace: God's Promise and Our Response*), reached its final form in May 1983 after going through three hotly debated drafts. The drafting process reflected divisions within and outside the Catholic Church: the letter coincided with a vigorous public debate of nuclear defense and deterrent policy

Given the spirited response to the nuclear pastoral, the bishops were braced for controversy in their new task. Early in the drafting process, they decided to shift the focus from a theoretical questioning of capitalism to a more concrete examination of the U.S. economy. They also proposed to study four main areas: employment, poverty, planning, and international trade. Later, food and agricultural policy appeared as a fifth topic for analysis.

The full text of the first draft was published under the title "Catholic Social Teaching and the U.S. Economy." Representative excerpts, as published in the *New York Times,* are reproduced here along with early critiques and part of a letter written by a lay Catholic group in anticipation of the bishops' draft. To put the question of Catholic teaching on social issues in the proper historical perspective, portions of a Labor Day statement by Archbishop of New York John J. O'Connor have been included as an appendix. The archbishop's remarks summarize the tradition of Catholic social teaching and the several levels of moral authority that exist in documents like pastoral letters.

The bishops will be debating the proposals in this draft for most of 1985, if not longer, before voting to approve a definitive text. If the process of drafting the nuclear pastoral is any guide, there will be substantial alterations and additions. With this draft, however, the U.S. Catholic bishops have initiated a debate on economic policy that will continue long after publication of the final version.

The Ethics and Public Policy Center is publishing these essays in the hope that they will contribute to this ongoing debate about moral, social, and economic issues that affect us all.

In all Center publications the views expressed are those of the authors.

ROBERT ROYAL, *Research Associate*
Ethics and Public Policy Center

Washington, D.C.
February 1985

Catholic Social Teaching and the U.S. Economy

Excerpts From the First Draft

U.S. CATHOLIC BISHOPS

THE POOR HAVE a special claim on our concern because they are vulnerable and needy. We believe that all—Christians, Jews, those of other faiths or no faith at all—must measure their actions and choices by what they do *for* and *to* the poor. As pastors and as citizens we are convinced of one fundamental criterion for economic decisions, policies, and institutions: They must all be at the service of human beings. The economy was made for people, *all* people, and not the other way around.

Everyone knows the significance of economic policy, economic organizations, and economic relationships, a significance that goes beyond purely secular or technical questions to profoundly human, and therefore moral, matters. It touches our very faith in God and what we hope and believe about the destiny of humanity. The signs of our time direct the pastoral concern of the church to these moral aspects of economic activity. Interpreting this activity in the light of the Gospel—at the local, national, and international levels—is the task we have set for ourselves in this pastoral letter.

In this effort to discern the signs of the times in U.S. economic life we have listened to many ways of analyzing the problems and many proposed solutions. In our discussion, study, and reflection, one thing has become evident. There is no clear consensus about the nature of the problems facing the country or about the best ways to address these problems effectively.

Reprinted by permission of the U.S. Catholic Conference. The excerpts reproduced here—which constitute only a small portion of the 112-page letter—appeared in the *New York Times* on Monday, November 12, 1984. The full text is available from the U.S. Catholic Conference, 1312 Massachusetts Avenue N.W., Washington, D.C. 20005.

The nation wonders whether it faces fundamentally new economic challenges that call for major changes in its way of doing business or whether adjustments within the framework of existing institutions will suffice.

This uncertainty and alternation between hope and apprehension has many causes. The U.S. economy has been immensely successful in providing for the material needs and in raising the living standard of its citizens. Our nation is one of the richest on earth. Despite this great wealth the country has recently gone through a severe recession with the highest unemployment rates since the Great Depression of the 1930s. In the recovery from this painful period the situation has improved, but very serious doubts remain about the future. The rate of poverty has risen sharply in recent years and is now at the highest level since 1965. Unemployment is exceptionally high even in the midst of the recovery, especially for minorities and youth. Some regions have been especially hard hit and their economic futures are in doubt. Farmers with moderate-sized holdings, workers in aging heavy industries, owners of vulnerable small businesses, and the poor and minority population in many central cities are often tempted to despair.

Two Views of the Problem

Some analysts argue that these problems result from a fundamental structural transition in the U.S. economy caused by new international competition, the movement of labor-intensive industries out of the country, the displacement of jobs by advanced technology, and a shift from a manufacturing and industrial economy to a service economy with lower-paying jobs. Add to this a major threat to the stability of the international financial system posed by the huge debts of several developing countries. A deepening crisis would leave no one untouched.

Others see the situation in less dramatic terms. They recognize that very serious problems exist, such as the aging of the industrial base in cities of the northern and central regions of the country, the displacement of many farmers from the land, the large trade deficits which eliminate jobs in the United States, and the fraying of the social "safety net" which protects those at the bottom of society. But they consider these grave problems to be the result of particular policies that can be changed incrementally rather than as the sign of a deep shift in the nature of the economy. They believe, for example, that by reducing deficits, increasing productivity, taking remedial actions to assist declining cities, farms, and industries, and carefully managing and rescheduling the Third World debt, a crisis can be avoided within the framework of existing institutions.

The investment of human creativity and material resources in the production of the weapons of war only makes these economic problems more intractable. The rivalry and mutual fear between the superpowers channel resources away from the task of creating a more just and productive economy into a seemingly endless effort to create more powerful and technologically sophisticated weaponry.

Even more damaging from the viewpoint of economic justice are the arms races between developing countries and their neighbors. Poor countries can ill afford to use their scarce resources to buy weapons when they lack food, education, and health care for large parts of their population.

One thing is certain in all this discussion: The stakes are enormously high. U.S. economic institutions and policies directly affect the dignity and well-being of millions of U.S. citizens. Choices made here have worldwide effects. Decisions made abroad have immediate consequences in the lives of U.S. citizens. How our country responds to the economic problems it faces will help or harm people all around the globe.

Morality and Economics

We are well aware of the difficulties involved in relating moral and religious values to economic life. Modern society has become so complex and fragmented that people have difficulty sensing the relationship among the different dimensions of their lives, such as the economic, the moral, and the religious. During the preparation of this letter we have often been asked what possible connection there could be between Christian morality and the technical questions of economic policy. We acknowledge the problem of discovering these links, and we also fully accept the fact that social and economic affairs "enjoy their own laws and values which must be gradually deciphered, put to use, and regulated by human beings." Religious and moral conviction cannot, simply by itself, produce solutions to economic dilemmas. We are confident, however, that the Christian moral tradition can make an important contribution to finding the right path. In the words of the Second Vatican Council:

> This split between the faith which many profess and their daily lives deserves to be counted among the more serious errors of our age. Long since, the prophets of the Old Testament fought vehemently against this

scandal, and even more did Jesus Christ himself in the New Testament threaten it with grave consequences.

We write with two purposes. The first is to provide guidance for members of our own church as they seek to form their consciences and reach moral decisions about economic matters. The second is to add our voice to the public debate about U.S. economic policies. In pursuing the first of these purposes, we argue from a distinctively Christian perspective that has been shaped by the Bible and by the content of Christian tradition, and from a standpoint that reflects our faith in God: Father, Son, and Holy Spirit. The second purpose demands that our arguments be developed in a reasoned manner that will be persuasive to those who do not share our faith or our tradition.

New Commitment to Economic Justice

Both the diversity of the U.S. Catholic community and the church's extension across national borders present a unique challenge to us in preparing this letter, charged as we are with the ministry of fostering unity. Economic divisions and conflicts between persons, within our country and on a world scale, can threaten both the unity of the human family and the unity of the church. Therefore we want to call all persons, no matter what their income or status, to a new commitment to economic justice. Such a commitment is an inescapable implication of belief in Jesus Christ. From a perspective shaped by the Gospel, no one can turn a deaf ear to the voice of the poor. No one can claim the name Christian and at the same time acquiesce in the hunger and homelessness that exists around the world and in our own country. We intend this letter to be an invitation and a challenge to those in our church who may be tempted to a narrower perspective.

John Paul II has summoned the church to be a community of disciples, a community in which "we must see first and foremost Christ saying to each member of the community: Follow me." When the first followers of Jesus heard and answered this call they left all things to become one with Jesus in the mystery of the cross.

In many areas of church life, to be a follower of Christ demands suffering and renunciation. Questions of family life, sexual morality, and war and peace face Catholics of the United States with challenges that summon them to the deepest commitment of faith. This is no less true in the area of economics and social justice. We live in one of the most affluent cultures in history where many of the values of an increasingly materialistic society stand in direct conflict with the gospel vision. We have been exhorted by John Paul II to break with "the frenzy of consumerism" and to adopt a "simple way of living." Our contemporary prosperity exists alongside the poverty of many both at home and abroad, and the image of disciples who "left all" to follow Jesus is difficult to reconcile with a contemporary ethos that encourages amassing as much as possible.

If the economy is to function in a way that respects the dignity of persons, these qualities should be present: It should enable persons to find a significant measure of self-realization in their labor; it should permit persons to fulfill their material needs through adequate remuneration; and it should make possible the enhancement of unity and solidarity within the family, the nation, and the world community.

Failures of U.S. Society

While the United States can be rightfully proud of its achievements as a society, we know full well that there have been failures, some of them massive and ugly. Hunger persists in our country, as our church-sponsored soup kitchens testify. Far too many people are homeless and must seek refuge from the cold in our church basements. As pastors we know the despair that can devastate individuals, families, and whole communities when the plague of unemployment strikes. Inadequate funding for education puts a high mortgage on our economic future. Racial discrimination has devastating effects on the economic well-being of minorities. Inequality in employment opportunity, low wages for women, and lack of sufficient child-care services can undermine family life.

Overcoming these obstacles will be an onerous task. It must begin with the formation of a new cultural consensus that *all persons really do have rights in the economic sphere* and that society has a moral obligation to take the necessary steps to ensure that no one among us is hungry, homeless, unemployed, or otherwise denied what is necessary to live with dignity.

The citizenry of the United States needs a new and stronger will to pursue this task in a sustained way in the years ahead. It will be an undertaking which involves struggle: a struggle for greater understanding, a struggle with our own selfishness, and a struggle to develop institutions that support active participation in economic life for all. The effort to guarantee the economic rights of all will face resistance until the fullness of the kingdom of God has been established by God's gracious initiative. Until that day arrives,

Christ calls us to the conversion of heart which will enable us to engage in this struggle with courage and hope.

We believe the time has come for [an] . . .experiment in economic democracy: the creation of an order that guarantees the minimum conditions of human dignity in the economic sphere for every person. By drawing on the resources of the Catholic moral-religious tradition, we hope to make a contribution to such a new "American experiment" in this letter.

We believe that the level of inequality in income and wealth in our society and even more the inequality on the world scale today must be judged morally unacceptable.

'Option for the Poor'

The fulfillment of the basic needs of the poor is of the highest priority. Personal decisions, social policies, and power relationships must all be evaluated by their effects on those who lack the minimum necessities of nutrition, housing, education, and health care. Our society has to consider other goals than these, such as productivity and economic efficiency, but not to the further detriment of the disadvantaged of our world. This evaluation of decisions, policies, and institutions primarily in light of their impact on the poor constitutes the "preferential option for the poor" which flows from biblical faith. It is also a priority fully supported by human experience and reason. In particular, this principle grants priority to meeting fundamental human needs over the fulfillment of desires for luxury consumer goods or for profits that do not ultimately benefit the common good of the community.

Increased economic participation for the marginalized takes priority over the preservation of privileged concentrations of power, wealth, and income. This principle follows from the fact that economic rights and responsibilities must find expression in the institutional order of society. It grants priority to policies and programs that enhance participation through work. It also points out the need for policies to improve the situation of groups unjustly discriminated against in the past. And it has very important implications for the institutions that shape the international economic order.

Meeting human needs and increasing participation should be priority targets in the investment of wealth, talent, and human energy. Increasing productivity both in the United States and in less developed parts of the world is a clear need. But different sorts of investment of human and financial resources can have very different outcomes for people even when they have similar rates of productivity. This principle presents a strong moral challenge to policies that put large amounts of talent and capital into the production of luxury consumer goods and military technology while failing to invest sufficiently in education, in the basic infrastructure of our society, or in economic sectors that produce the jobs, goods, and services that we urgently need.

Unions may. . . legitimately resort to strikes in situations where they are the only available means for pursuing the justice owed to workers. No one may deny the right to organize for purposes of collective bargaining or coercively suppress unions without attacking human dignity itself. Therefore we firmly oppose organized efforts, such as those regrettably now seen in this country, to break existing unions or to prevent workers from organizing through intimidation and threats. U.S. labor-law reform is needed to give greater substance to the right to organize, to prevent intimidation of workers, and to provide remedies in a more timely manner for unfair labor practices.

The Right to Own

[The] support of private ownership does not mean that any individual, group, organization, or nation has the right to unlimited accumulation of wealth. Especially when there are so many needy people in our world, the right to own must bow to the higher principles of stewardship and the common use of the goods of creation. There is a "social mortgage" on private property which implies that "private property does not constitute for anyone an absolute or unconditioned right."

The church's teaching opposes collectivist and statist economic approaches. But it also resists the notion that an unimpeded market automatically produces justice.

We measure the justice of our economic institutions in part by their ability to deliver those goods and services which fulfill basic human needs and provide a living worthy of human dignity. In our economy, consumption is a stimulus to production, and increased production generates employment. As consumers, therefore, all of us play an important role in the pursuit of economic justice.

Nevertheless, both our Christian faith and the norms of human justice impose distinct limits on what we consume and how we view material goods. The Gospel calls us to renounce disordered attachment to earthly possessions. Jesus blessed the poor, though he did not teach that degrading poverty is somehow a blessed condition. He called us to seek first the kingdom of God rather than an ever increasing store of goods and wealth. Similarly, the earliest Christians sought to alleviate poverty and called upon the wealthy in their community to relinquish their goods in the service of their brothers and sisters. Such limits on consumption and the accumulation of wealth are essential if we are to avoid what Pope Paul VI called "the most evident form of moral underdevelopment," namely avarice. They are also essential to the realization of the justice that protects human dignity.

All U.S. citizens, especially parents, must nurture the inner freedom to resist these pressures constantly to seek more. Also, men and women in the advertising and marketing field must examine the methods they use to see if they can really stand scrutiny in this light. During his visit to our country, Pope John Paul II challenged us to recognize the urgency of our responsibility, "even if it involves a notable change in the attitudes and life styles of those blessed with a larger share of the world's goods."

A consumerist mentality which encourages immediate gratification mortgages our future and ultimately risks undermining the foundations of a just order. Both our cultural values and our tax structures need to be revised to discourage excessively high levels of consumption and to encourage saving and consequent investment in both private and public endeavors that promote the economic rights of all persons.

All the moral principles that govern the just operation of any economic endeavor apply to the church and its many agencies and institutions.

The principles of Catholic social teaching provide a rich tradition from which to approach a discussion of economic justice. They form the basis for the reflections on specific public issues that will be addressed in this section. We shall attempt here to focus the light of moral principles on certain of the economic realities and choices that are central to American life.

In doing so, we are aware that the movement from principle to practice is a complex and sometimes difficult task. We undertake this task with the firm conviction that moral values have an important role to play in determining public policies, but with the understanding that ethical principles in themselves do not dictate specific kinds of programs or provide blueprints for action.

Commitment to Full Employment

We recommend that the nation make a major new policy commitment to achieve full employment. We believe that an unemployment rate in the range of 3 or 4 per cent is a reasonable definition of full employment in the United

States today. We have noted above that considerably higher rates have received growing public and professional acceptance in recent years for a number of reasons: demographic changes, institutional rigidities, and employment/inflation tradeoffs. In light of the possibilities for reducing unemployment and the criteria for doing so successfully, we believe that 6 to 7 per cent unemployment is unacceptable and is not the best the United States can do.

We recommend increased support by the government for direct job-creation programs targeted on the structurally unemployed. Such programs can take the form of direct public-service employment and also of public subsidies for employment in the private sector.

The United States has no shortage of major needs which are not likely to be met unless we take concerted public action. Our roads and bridges need to be repaired, farmland needs to be conserved and restored, parks and recreation facilities need to be improved, low-cost housing needs to be built, and our public transportation system needs to be expanded. Private industry must play a major role in meeting these needs through ordinary contractual relations with government. Direct public-service employment programs also have a role to play in the effort.

We recommend expansion of apprenticeship and job-training programs in the private sector which are administered and supported jointly by business, labor unions, and government.

One much discussed condition that does not appear to be either a cause or a cure of poverty is personal motivation. Some claim that the poor are poor because they do not try hard enough to find a job, do not work hard enough when they have one, and generally do not try to get ahead. In fact, one of the most detailed studies ever done on poverty in this country showed that initial attitudes were not an important predictor of later income. Indeed, some of those who worked the longest hours remained poor because of low wages. Until there is real evidence that motivation significantly contributes to poverty, this kind of argument should be abandoned. It is not only unsupported but is insulting to the poor.

The Nature of Poverty

Here we cannot enter into a full discussion of the nature of poverty, but we want to raise a few central points. Poverty is not merely the lack of adequate financial resources. To be poor entails a more profound kind of deprivation, for it means being denied full participation in the economic, social, and political life of society. It means being without sufficient control over and access to the decisions that affect your life. It means being marginal-ized and powerless in a way that assaults not only your pocketbook but also your fundamental human dignity.

Our nation's response to poverty, therefore, must not only include improve-ments in welfare programs for the poor, as we shall discuss below. It must also address broader social and institutional factors that are an integral part of this problem. We call attention here to three such factors: racial discrimi-nation, the feminization of poverty, and the distribution of income and wealth.

If the United States were a country in which poverty existed amidst rela-tively equitable income distribution, one might argue that we do not have the resources to provide everyone with an adequate living. But, in fact, this is a country marked by glaring disparities of wealth and income.

Catholic social teaching does not suggest that absolute equality in the dis-tribution of income and wealth is required. Some degree of inequality is not only acceptable, but may be desirable for economic and social reasons. How-ever, gross inequalities are morally unjustifiable, particularly when millions lack even the basic necessities of life. In our judgment, the distribution of income and wealth in the United States is so inequitable that it violates this minimum standard of distributive justice.

Need for Welfare Reform

For millions of poor Americans the only economic safety net is the pub-lic welfare system. We believe that programs in this area are essential and should be designed to serve the needs of the poor in a manner that respects their human dignity. In our judgment the present welfare system does not meet that criterion and is in need of major reform.

In general our welfare system is woefully inadequate. It is a patchwork arrangement marked by benefit levels that leave recipients poor; gaps in coverage; inconsistent treatment of poor people in similar situations; wide variations in benefits across states; humiliating treatment of clients; and fre-quent complaints about "red tape."

One reason why we do not have a humane welfare system is our punitive attitude toward the poor. Americans have a tendency to blame poverty on laziness, to stigmatize welfare recipients, to exaggerate the benefits actually received by the poor, and to overstate the extent of fraud in welfare payments. The belief persists in this country that the poor are poor by choice, that anyone can escape poverty by hard work, and that welfare programs make it easier for people to avoid work. Hence we devise progams that single out the poor for special treatment, provide meager benefits, and are often demeaning in the way they are administered. In violation of the spirit of solidarity, the needy are kept at the edge of society and told in dozens of ways that they are a burden.

Within the limits just stated, public-assistance programs should encourage rather than penalize gainful employment.

Eligibility for public assistance should also not depend on work requirements or work tests.

The design of public-assistance programs should involve the participation of the recipient population and avoid or minimize stigma to clients.

The administration of public-assistance programs should show respect for clients. With the punitive spirit behind our present welfare programs, a premium is often put on deterring applications, using regulations to create difficulties for clients, and otherwise showing the poor that they are not to be trusted. Such practices seldom occur in most social benefit programs for the non-poor.

The damage done to the poor through the present administrative system, which often pits case worker against client in an adversarial relationship, far outweighs any putative savings in welfare expenses.

Need for North-South Dialogue

We do not intend to evaluate the various proposals for international economic reform or to provide a blueprint for a new international system. Rather we want to urge a basic and overriding consideration: that both empirical and moral evidence, especially the precarious situation of the developing countries, calls for the renewal of the dialogue urged by Pope John Paul II between North and South. We strongly recommend that such a dialogue aim at restructuring the existing patterns of economic relations so as to establish greater equity and meet the basic human needs of the poor people of the South.

In recent years U.S. policy toward the developing world has shifted from its earlier emphasis on basic human needs and social and economic development to a selective assistance based on an East-West assessment of a North-South set of problems. Such a view makes the principal policy issue one of "national security," which in turn is described in political-military terms. Developing countries thus become largely test cases in the East-West struggle; they have meaning or value only in terms of the larger geopolitical calculus. The result is that issues of political and economic development take second place to the political-strategic argument. We deplore this change.

In our view, however, the most damaging single retrenchment is the decline in the U.S. support for the International Development Association (I.D.A.), the "soft loan window" of the World Bank. Its clients are countries whose per capita income is $410 per year or less. Through a series of recent policy decisions the United States has shifted its role in I.D.A. from being a leading supporter of the poorest countries to becoming an obstacle to multilateral efforts to help poor people in these countries.

In 1982 the military expenditures of the developed countries were seventeen times larger than their foreign assistance; in 1984 the United States alone budgeted more than twenty times as much for defense as for foreign assistance, and nearly two-thirds of the latter took the form of military assistance or went to countries because of their perceived security value to the United States. Rather than promoting U.S. arms sales to countries that cannot afford them, we should be campaigning for an international agreement to reduce this lethal trade.

The international economic order is in crisis; the gap between rich and poor countries and between rich and poor people within countries is widening. The United States represents the most powerful single factor in the international economic equation. With that kind of power comes a commensurate responsibility. But even as we speak of crisis, we see an opportunity for the United States to launch, on both a national and a global scale, a campaign for economic democracy and justice to match the still incomplete but encouraging political democracy we have achieved here with so much pain and sacrifice.

Global Affirmative Action

To restructure the international order along lines of greater equity and participation will require a far more stringent application of the principles of affirmative action than we have seen in the United States itself. Like the struggle for political democracy at home, it will entail sacrifices. But that is what the recognition and acceptance of responsibility means. As a nation founded on Judeo-Christian religious principles, we are called to make those sacrifices in order to bring justice and peace to the world, as well as for our own long-term self-interest. The times call for the kinds of leadership and vision that have characterized our nation in the past when the choices were clear. Now we need to call upon these qualities again. As Pope John Paul II said to President Carter during his visit to the United States, "America, which in the past decades had demonstrated goodness and generosity in providing food for the hungry of the world, will, I am sure, be able to match this generosity with an equally convincing contribution to the establishing of a world order that will create the necessary economic and trade conditions for a more just relationship between all the nations of the world."

We hope that this letter has begun to clarify how Catholic social teaching applies to the situations we are describing, so that our country can move in the direction the Pope indicated. We share his conviction that many of these issues generally called economic are, at root, moral and therefore require the application of moral principles derived from the Gospels and from the evolving social teaching of the church.

There are indeed different paths to holiness in the church and vocations to different forms of sharing in the effort to achieve the goals presented in this letter. These reflections on worship and liturgy, however, make vividly clear that none of us can afford to live a spiritually schizophrenic existence in which our private lives are oriented toward Christian discipleship while our economic activities are devoid of these same values.

Toward the Future

Excerpts

LAY COMMISSION ON
CATHOLIC SOCIAL TEACHING AND THE U.S. ECONOMY

EVERY HUMAN SOCIETY must strike a proper balance between individual liberty and common action. The American experiment has entailed a keen struggle to find that balance. On the one side is the unique commitment of our people to personal liberty, as enshrined in and animating the federal Constitution. On the other is the central presupposition of that historical document: that our vigorous familial and communal life continue healthy and strong, a common unity. Strong families and strong communities teach those personal virtues without which the Constitution cannot be preserved, and provide care for those who are in need of help and guidance. *E pluribus unum*: One out of many.

Today, that sense of balance is sometimes lacking in the language of those who either choose individual liberty over all other concerns, and hence embrace a kind of radical individualism, or seek to enlarge the power and scope of government, and hence embrace a kind of statist meddlesomeness. Catholic social thought has from the first sought to avoid the "double danger" (Pius XI) of individualism and collectivism. It holds firm three basic principles: the sacred dignity of the person, the social nature of human life, and the obligation to assign social decisions to the level of authority best suited to take them.

In recent decades, Catholic thought has been deeply influenced by the American experience, often almost unconsciously. It has also, to a degree

Reprinted by permission. The commission, a group of Catholic layman led by William Simon and Michael Novak, produced "Toward the Future" in anticipation of the bishops' draft letter. These excerpts reduce by nearly one-half Part III of the lay letter. The full text is available from the Lay Commission on Catholic Social Teaching and the U.S. Economy, P.O. Box 364, North Tarrytown, N.Y. 10591.

which will probably increase in the future, helped to shape the American experience. To understand the reciprocal relation between thought and experience, we begin by reviewing the principles of that thought and the history of that experience.

Thus, in Part I, we survey the principles of Catholic social thought, and examine the great significance of the American experiment for Catholic social thought. Catholics on other continents have scarcely noted this significance. It was clear to our U.S. Catholic forebears a century ago, and it is clear to us.

In Part II, we reflect on the lay vocation of co-creation, especially as it is now being lived by millions of lay persons in economic activities. Placing the theme of creation at the center of his teaching on economic justice, Pope John Paul II has suggested that it is the vocation of humans, made in the image of the Creator, to unlock the secrets the Creator has hidden in creation, and thus to move history toward the fulfillment of the Creator's marvelous designs. So, too, political economies should liberate the creative energies of every human person within them. This liberal democracies set out to do.

In Part III, we face five serious problem areas in the U.S. economy: (1) the family; (2) poverty and welfare; (3) job creation; (4) free trade and global interdependence; and (5) social cooperation and providence. While we do not propose programmatic solutions, we do call attention to areas requiring imagination and fresh initiatives. It is the glory of systems such as ours that they are always open to reform and, like the Church itself, *semper reformanda*. These words of Pius XII in 1951 express our vision:

> True religion and profound humaneness are not rivals. They are sisters. They have nothing to fear from one another, but everything to gain. Let each remain loyal to the law of its being, while it respects the vital needs and varied outward manifestations of the other, and the resultant harmonizing of two forces will endow any people engaged in the fulfillment of its appointed tasks with the most valuable incentives to real prosperity and solid progress.[3]

III. Improving the U.S. Economy

1. THE FAMILY

One of the elements of Catholic belief which we on the Lay Commission most admire, and for which we are most grateful, is the Catholic emphasis on the family. The family is the most important institution in our lives. Normally, it is in and through the family that the Faith is taught and practiced. To be sure, even the family often falls from its own high ideals. Nonetheless, those ideals are crucial to our lives, both as persons and as citizens of a reliably functioning political economy. In the family, more often than not, we see the Word of God lived by those we most love and admire. In death and in sickness, in good times and in bad, more often than not, the family is steadfast. When things go well in our families, adversities in the world are supportable. When things go badly in our families, even successes in the world do not bring happiness.

In important ways, the family is the center of human happiness and striving. The family is made in the image of the Trinity, a community of persons, and in the image of the Creator, from whom all new life springs. It offers us, as well, our first images of Providence, teaching us as children a certain basic trust in reality and in creation's God; and teaching us, as adults, our duty to provide for those entrusted to our care and love. The family is the first teacher of social justice.

Christian life is first lived and learned in families. The family is the training ground of virtue: of an alert and questioning attitude; of habits of hard work, honesty, and responsibility; of cooperation, trust, and conviviality; of courtesy, kindness, and forgiveness; of boldness, inventiveness, and daring. The family is the nurturer of realism, against utopianism of all sorts. It is in the family that we learn the difference between romantic love and realistic love, between our fantasies about ourselves and the sharp edges which our spouses and our children see in us, between illusions and hard-won honesty. Family life teaches us to care for others, to forgive and to seek forgiveness. As it was in the families given to us and under the care of our own parents that we learned the fundamental virtues, personal and social, on which integrity and hard work and fidelity are based, so it is also in the families we have founded, among our own children, that we attempt to pass on these same virtues, down that long human chain which has come to be known as tradition. No economic order can ever be any stronger than the virtues of its citizens. In that sense, the family is the cradle of a strong economy. It carries forward the virtues, values, skills, practical lore, and material achievements of the past and the present, in an orderly and personal way, into the future.

It is no accident, either, that totalitarians who aim to destroy every liberty and rip out any vestige of loyalty to truth seek first of all to infiltrate, weaken, and destroy the integrity of the family, sowing mistrust and suspicion even in this haven of the human heart. One can understand neither democracy nor a market economy respectful of private property apart from a sound structure of family life, in which families are independent of the state both politically and economically, and in which the state may not violate family rights, including those of property. Too often concerned with the two novel realities of modern political life, the individual and the state, political economists have tended to overlook the centrality of the family. As a traditional institution, some have neglected it as pre-modern; others have unconsciously taken it for granted, without sufficient attention to its importance. Both in personal life and in the reliable functioning of healthy political economies, the family is a crucial institution. It is a bridge between personal morality and social morality, the privileged school both of personal virtues and of social virtues, without which neither personal life nor political economy can long prosper.

Serious questions arise, therefore, concerning four factors in American life which injure family life, or make family life more difficult. Limiting ourselves simply to those factors which appear in the economic system, we observe the following.

First, the financial situation of young families today is quite different from those of their parents or grandparents. Most young couples starting out in marriage today strain to meet the high purchase price of a first home. More formidable still, mortgage interest rates are extremely high. There are compensating factors on the income side of this equation: both husband and wife are likely to be working, and for higher real wages at their age than any prior generation. They are likely to begin with considerably more in family and in educational assets than those with which previous generations began. The home owned by their parents is likely to have appreciated significantly in value, thus giving the family as a whole a far stronger balance sheet than it had a generation or two ago. Nonetheless, current high prices and high interest rates provide the younger generation today with obstacles as difficult, in their way, as those their parents and grandparents faced years ago.

Second, with respect to a much-neglected matter, we object to those base forms of commerce—in abortion, pornography, prostitution, and drugs— which make direct war upon the virtues of family life and on the necessary moral strength of any free republic. We call upon business leaders to become critically aware of the moral impact, explicit and implicit, of their own advertising and of the entertainments they support. In our time, entertainment has become a main teacher of values, entering the home itself—and with far too little examination of its moral quality.

Third, one of the crucial pillars of family life is economic independence and self-reliance. In this context, Catholic social teaching has long upheld the principle of the living wage—that wage, proportionate to circumstances, which allows each family a decent measure of income and security against the common hazards of human life. In more affluent societies such as ours, the concept of aspiring to a better life has been added to the older concept of the living wage. For standards of health care, education, opportunity, and possibilities for "the pursuit of happiness" have been raised to historically unprecedented levels. Considerably more than the sort of sufficiency just above subsistence levels which was sought so desperately by even our recent ancestors is now sought by most couples, even those who cherish, by today's standards, a "simple" way of life. Indeed, in many families today, one job alone is not judged sufficient; spouses and older children also wish to work, not only out of economic necessity but even for reasons of personal satisfaction, growth in experience, and fulfillment.

Fourth, one of the great advantages of a system such as ours is that, generation by generation, it raises its standards of what can and ought to be done. The economic system is so amazingly productive that it often tempts society to place ever greater burdens upon it. The danger, of course, is that such burdens finally may destroy it. Nonetheless, in our time, with large numbers of wives joining their husbands in paid employment, and with many hard-pressed single parents also seeking work, yet a new burden is already being met by many businesses, small and large. Some provide child care on their premises. Others, when possible, arrange work schedules for the convenience of family schedules. We applaud these developments, where they are practical.

The very successes of our economy generate ever-new problems with every new advance. Family life is so important both to individuals and to the republic that the various institutions of the U.S. economy would be well advised to make it central in their strategies for self-improvement.

2. POVERTY AND WELFARE

One measure of a good society is how well it cares for the weakest and most vulnerable of its members. Historically, the first challenge of the liberal economy was to create such new wealth as would raise standards of living for all citizens steadily over time. The historical transition from agrarian-mercantilistic economies, to the liberal economies of the nineteenth century, to the combination of free-market and welfare economies of today, involved many long and bitter struggles. In the brief two hundred years of this vast social transformation, life has been vastly improved for the poor, the weak, and the vulnerable. Even domestically, however, this transformation is unfinished.

On the one hand, there is a temptation for citizens in free economies committed to generous welfare programs to go too far in enhancing the power of the central state. On the other hand, a Jewish and Christian society will wish to help the poor. Philosophically, the problem is twofold: how to help the poor and the needy without generating an incapacitating dependency.

Those of the poor who cannot be self-reliant should be distinguished from those who with a little help, training, and incentives can achieve self-reliance. For the latter, choosing wise policies—which actually help both the poor and the common good—is a high moral imperative. It is exceedingly difficult of achievement.

The generosity of the American people in wishing to help the poor, by supporting legislation specifically targeted on the needs of the poor of both types, has been immense. Let us observe, not as a policy recommendation, but as a way of measuring the magnitude of the problem, that more money is actually spent directly on the poor each year (more than $100 billion) than would be required, if distributed directly to the poor, to lift every man, woman, and child among them above the poverty level. That this has not actually been achieved is *prima facie* evidence of faulty design in poverty programs. From the beginning, these were intended to enhance "the integrity and preservation of the family unit." This generous aim, too, has scarcely been achieved; quite the opposite.

In New York City alone, according to a recent report, 37 per cent of all live births during 1983 were illegitimate, and in some areas the percentage was far higher. The resulting disadvantage is weighty. Whereas 36 per cent of families headed by women are poor, only 8 per cent of "intact families"—those with two parents—are poor. Children born out of wedlock are far more likely to be poorly educated and poorly prepared for employment, likely to acquire habits of dependency and unemployment.

One cannot say that poverty causes illegitimacy, for during earlier eras of far greater poverty among Americans there was much less illegitimacy. Public opinion is now tolerant of illegitimacy, as earlier it was not. The consequences are devastating.

Some say that joblessness and a lack of sense of self-worth make young men less responsible than in the past. Yet is is surely wrong for public commentators to increase this sense of personal worthlessness, if it exists, by denying to human beings a sense of personal responsibility for their deeds. Whatever else it may be, illegitimacy is a moral disorder. To try to shift all blame to others, to external conditions, or to "society" is to deny persons their own inherent worth as moral agents. To treat human persons solely as "victims," as if they had no moral responsibility of their own, is to treat them as less than human. For this reason, all who play a role as moral leaders in our society have a serious obligation to insist upon the moral responsibility of every single person, of every class and station.

Illegitimacy is an issue of personal and public morality, as well as an issue requiring social action on the part of the entire society. Young persons must be taught that illegitimacy saddles children with an unusually difficult future. After the fact, nonetheless, community support must be forthcoming, to turn tragedy to hope. As to how best to achieve that, without doing more harm than good, reasonable persons of good will frequently disagree. Solving that problem, though, is crucial to all involved.

We believe firmly that the poor must be assisted in their efforts to climb out of poverty. Monetarily, the sum needed to wipe out poverty—the "poverty shortfall"—is not large by federal standards. Indeed, state and local governments and private sources already contribute, with the federal government, to that task. If the poverty shortfall of $45 billion were simply *given* to the poor, that would of course temporarily lift all above the poverty line as defined by the Census Bureau. This observation, which is not a policy recommendation, forces us to see that the magnitude of the problem, sheerly as a monetary problem, is not great. Poverty is more a *human* than a monetary problem. Helping the poor to acquire the skills of productive economic independence demands far more from us than mere monetary grants.

There are several points we would like to make, in particular, about poverty among blacks. Since poverty has human and cultural dimensions, no one can discount the effects upon some blacks of generations of slavery, followed by generations of being looked down upon and shunted into menial positions. The sharpest indication of such effects is suggested by the fact that American blacks who experienced slavery in the West Indies have shown much higher self-esteem as well as higher success rates in school, in household income, and in public leadership than those who experienced the slavery of the American South. The difference seems to lie in this: in the West Indies, many blacks were encouraged to pursue education, drawn into a large variety of professions and occupations, and even as field hands rewarded through the incentive system. By contrast, in the American South, education was often discouraged, slaves were kept out of occupations promising advancement, and incentives for better work were few. Such systemic differences have critical spiritual consequences. We admire the amazing resilience of the human spirit, not only in the remarkable achievements of black Americans but also in the good spirit they bring to American public and private life.

As we have noted, there are roughly 24 million white poor, compared to roughly 10 million black poor; nonetheless, 62 per cent of the "persistently poor" are black (living predominantly in the South). And about 35 per cent of all poor persons, including those only temporarily poor, are black. Thus, it is wrong to think of poverty as merely a problem for blacks—the white poor outnumber the black poor by more than 2:1. Nonetheless, the human dimensions of poverty rub the black poor much more harshly. The spirit is battered every day by feelings of discrimination as well as by poverty.

Considerations of this sort lead us to believe that Father James Naughton was correct when he testified before us, stressing the enormous amount of personal time and personal care it takes to bring some individuals born in poverty to economic self-reliance. Too many people want to entrust the problems of the poor to the government, and then forget about them. Many will give large amounts of money, vote for higher government aid—the only thing they will *not* do is be seen among the poor, helping the poor, person-to-person, family-to-family. Since poverty has a human dimension, far more basic than a monetary dimension, it would be less than Christian to speak of it solely as a question of system or structure, while ignoring the need one human being has for respect, attention, and realistic love from another. Those who say that person-to-person work is "remedial," "insignificant compared to structural changes," and "evasive" need to ask themselves why so many of the "structural reforms" and "systemic changes" they have put in place during the past twenty years seem to have made the human dimensions of poverty in America so much more harsh, isolating, and debilitating. Those who claim to speak for the poor do not always help the poor. While we admire governmental efforts to assist the poor, and believe that such assistance should continue, we believe that a more humane and personal effort is also in order.

In this necessary enterprise, the tradition of American voluntary associations—in neighborhood churches, schools, fraternal organizations, and other cooperatives—should be given far more attention in the way we think about public policy. The resources of a free people, banding together to meet their own needs in self-reliance, spring from a powerful American tradition. Poverty is not primarily a problem for the state. It is a *personal* and a *community* problem which each of us and all our appropriate associations, not only the state, ought to address. Government programs are important, but they are not sufficient. They are most successful when they empower citizens and local associations to solve their own problems.

Many of us would like to see our churches involve us in a more immediate way, person-to-person, in meeting the problems of the poor. The Catholic Church in the United States has some 19,000 parishes. Many have adopted sister parishes in poorer areas. Many offer food kitchens, child care, and practical instructional programs. Catholic parish and diocesan schools have made immense contributions in helping the poor, even many today who are not Catholics. Yet most parishes do not draw sufficiently upon the entrepreneurial and managerial skills of their parishioners. Some who work with the disadvantaged view their work as a holding action rather than as creative and productive. When others speak of "change," they often think in terms of state action, breeding more dependency, rather than in terms of launching new enterprises and creating new jobs, thus using the liberties and productive talents of a dynamic economy.

3. Employment Generation

One of the most pressing tasks of co-creation in every economy of the world is the creation of new jobs. For this, capital investment, enterprise, and social intelligence are needed. The transition from mercantilism to capitalism appeared when wealthy persons began to shift their wealth from personal consumption (palaces, private armies, balls, and the like) and began to invest it in productive enterprises. Such enterprises then began to employ the formerly idle, and to generate wages which raised the living standards of workers. Thus, the creation of wealth is simultaneously a social and a personal good. It helps the creator of wealth; it helps others—and the society as a whole. This is why the popes have in recent years criticized the Third World wealthy who do not invest in their own countries. (We note, though, the moral dilemma of persons of virtue who would like to invest in their own country, yet find its political economy wracked by inflation, instability, and uncertainty. This is yet another indication of the way in which even a virtuous people can be frustrated by an ill-designed system.)

If we consider only Latin America, a continent of massive unemployment and underemployment, it is clear that the task of job-creation is both indispensable and formidable. It is estimated that Latin America will need 76 million new jobs by the year 2000 just for those already born. Given rising populations, there is no way that all citizens in Latin America can be successfully employed in agricultural pursuits. The future of the poor of the world depends, therefore, upon a new explosion of entrepreneurial, commercial, and industrial activity. Most new employment must come from the creation of millions of small businesses.

So it is also in the United States. Employment in government (about 16 million) and in the *Fortune* 500 (about 14 million) has for some years been virtually static. An immense explosion of new jobs—some 26 million in all—has been created in the United States between 1970 and early 1984, and the majority of these have been created by small businesses. Enterprise is a major key to job creation.

In 1970, the total number of employed civilians in the United States was 78 million. In mid-1984, this number had climbed to 105 million. Such a record of job creation is unmatched by any other economy in the world, and is historically almost unprecedented. Since during this period the United States endured two large recessions—one in the mid-seventies, the other during 1979–82—this record is all the more remarkable.

Jobs do not simply happen, as fruit grows on trees; they must be created. New ideas are crucial in this creation. New waves of entrepreneurs must learn to look alertly for unmet needs—for new products and new services—and to invent new ways of meeting older needs. On all sides, we see much work to be done, not least in the very locations where there are large numbers of those who seek employment, where homes need to be restored and repainted, and where business starts are few, compelling local consumers to go elsewhere to meet their needs and to find employment. It is the task

of enterprising intellect to marry needed work to willing workers: to create
paying jobs where none existed before. In many places, chambers of commerce, associations of entrepreneurs, policy thinkers, and others are trying
to create a new environment for job creation. The fact, of course, is that just
as an artist cannot aim at beauty but must aim at producing a good body of
work, so jobs are an after-effect of creating goods and services.

There is much, of course, that government can do through its own macro-
economic and micro-economic policies. It must attend to the ways in which
it penalizes savings and prompts people to consume today rather than to invest in tomorrow. It must exercise intense vigilance to prevent inflation, and
it must strictly control its own expenditures and deficits.

4. Global Interdependence

The word *catholic* means universal, and we are conscious, in our vocation
as lay Catholics, of a universal bond of association with all human beings
on this planet, past, present, and future. Today all peoples are more inter-
dependent than ever before; it cannot be denied that this great achievement
has been brought into institutional being through the inventions of international transport, communications, trade, and finance pioneered by liberal
capitalist societies.

Over two hundred years ago Adam Smith was among the first to foresee,
desire, and encourage such global interdependence, imagining the development of the wealth of nations—all nations—united in lawlike, peaceful, mutual
relations of commerce and trade. The ancient word "commerce" (*commer-
cium*) suggests more than material exchange; in old hymns, it was used even
of the "admirable commerce" between God and humankind. Today, too,
world trade brings into being new forms of mutual understanding and new
voluntary relationships, and stimulates new ideas, international travel, and
an appetite for a more brotherly and sisterly world community.

Those nations and those parts of nations most closely drawn into international trade and international communications tend to be those of most
remarkable human development, not only in national wealth and per capita
income, but also in rising standards of longevity, infant mortality, health care,
education, and institutions of human rights. Those the more remote remain
to this day, whatever their admirable human qualities, the least likely to share
in modern vitalities, ideas, and benefits.

We recognize that culture differs from culture. Different peoples see and
do things differently according to their own histories and traditions. We have

experienced a remarkable pluralism within the Catholic Church, and we are led by it to respect pluralism in the world around us. We recognize the right of peoples to choose their own form of governance, through the consent of the governed, and to choose their own forms of culture and economic development. These rights are endowed by the Creator in individuals, not in states. Individuals in their associations are the seat of human rights; the Creator is their source. States have not created rights; God has. Thus, one great advantage we see in liberal societies—with their free economies, polities, and cultures—is that they are uniquely attuned to cultural pluralism. There are, to be sure, centripetal, homogenizing forces in modern technologies and means of communication, even as there are in the universality of science. Nonetheless, we deeply respect the cultural differences that add so much fecundity to human life. We reject all visions of a centrally directed world culture. We envisage a world of diverse cultures, amicably and peaceably related through mutual and voluntary association.

The economy of the United States is blessedly strong, with the dynamism that comes from liberty under law. What economic course ought the United States to set, to make our economy of maximum assistance to the poor of the world—we stress, the poor *people* of the world, rather than governments or nation-states?

There are two principles of international trade which we would like to stress. First, in today's world every nation has become dependent upon other nations. There is no longer any major economy which is totally independent.

The second principle is that, on the whole, and contrary to intuition, in open trade the weaker party often derives the greater benefits. This is so because the trade relation is typically of far greater importance to the weaker party. There are only a certain number of nations on this planet, for example, with which the United States *must* trade, in order to obtain vital goods or to maintain important markets. If the United States did not trade with the remaining nations, on which it depends but little, the loss to the United States would not be of as serious a consequence to the U.S. economy as the loss of U.S. markets would be to such weaker nations, which would be deeply injured. In this sense, the dependence of some nations upon the United States is considerably greater than the dependence of the United States upon them. This fact requires the people of the United States to be especially sensitive to the needs of such weaker trading partners. On the other hand, it must be noted that such dependency, where it exists, does not explain why such countries are poor; on the contrary, it points out how useful to their own development are open markets in the United States.

Since the era of world competition in the years ahead may be unlike the era we have known until now, we believe new policies are needed in manufacturing industries to protect workers who may be vulnerable to industry-wide economic change. Beyond customary policies already in effect—unemployment compensation, retraining programs, educational assistance, Trade Readjustment Allowances, and the like—we see the need for further practical invention. Two of the greatest burdens suddenly unemployed workers face are the loss of health insurance and an inability to meet mortgage payments. While we have not been in a position to cost out sound remedies to these necessities, we recognize the seriousness and probable persistence of the problem. The principle is that new means ought to be available to individual families and workers whose jobs are vulnerable through certain specifiable hazards of economic change. Change is today the law of international economics and contemporary inventiveness. Together with dynamic growth toward a better future for all come unavoidable losses for some, who deserve to have affordable means of self-protection. Social inventiveness must accompany technological inventiveness.

5. SOCIAL COOPERATION AND PROVIDENCE

The linchpin of both socialist and statist societies is "planning." That word is used in many different senses. Behind it usually lies a misleading intuition, viz., that if you take the brightest group of experts available, they can lay out an economic plan, whether compulsory or merely declarative, that will wisely marshall resources, eliminate waste, organize priorities, order sequences of action, dictate prices, establish wages, and so on in such a way that the whole economy would operate with optimum rationality. The model of rationality behind this word is that of mental guidance from above, as God the watchmaker was held by some philosophers to set the universe in motion.

The Catholic understanding of God is very different. God is pictured as Providence, allowing contingent causes to work in all their humanly baffling contingency, empowering human beings as free agents, compelling no one, but ordering all things sweetly and from within their own proper natures and liberties.

Drawing upon this image of God, we Catholic laypersons, free citizens of a free economy in a free republic, see quite clearly the importance of providence on the part of human beings: the role of stewardship, responsibility for the future, the duty to think ahead. If we value the social device of free markets, as we do, it is neither because we believe that markets embody irrationality and arbitrariness nor because we believe that markets exempt human beings from provident forethought. On the contrary, we value free markets because they allow for fresh insight, for new initiatives, for astringent criticism of their current deficiencies, and for new courses of action to bring about newly desired results. The image of some "Invisible Hand" distorts the reality of markets. Aside from the swift, objective, and indispensable information they give about real choices by real people, what is most valuable about markets is that they are open. Those concerned about stewardship, unmet needs, new necessities, and future requirements are able to enter markets and do new things. Markets, in short, allow for self-correction. They encourage habits of foresight and anticipation.

Markets are, then, a form of "rational" planning, whose rationality does not flow from the brains of a small group of authorities, but from the millions of acts of concrete intelligence performed by all who participate in them. The market is a kind of calculus of intelligent choices. Markets are a "rational" device, but not as small groups of experts are "rational."

In this respect, we have reflected on an observation made by Pope John Paul II in discussing planning:

As we view the whole human family throughout the world, we cannot fail to be struck by a disconcerting fact of immense proportions: the fact that while conspicuous natural resources remain unused, there are huge numbers of people who are unemployed or underemployed and countless multitudes of people suffering from hunger. This is a fact that without any doubt demonstrates that both within the individual political communities and in their relationships on the continental and world levels there is something wrong with the organization of work and employment, precisely at the most critical and socially most important points.

In our experience, these observations hold true most of all in those parts of the world in which markets do not function, individual intelligence is repressed, and human providence is frustrated.

In calling for "overall planning," as he does in the same place, John Paul II stresses the liberties we think crucial:

In the final analysis this overall concern weighs on the shoulders of the state, but it cannot mean one-sided centralization by the public authorities. Instead, what is in question is a just and rational coordination, within the framework of which the initiative of individuals, free groups and local work centers and complexes must be safeguarded.

We are skeptical of entrusting planning to the state, for we see no government on this planet whose capacity wholly to direct free men and women we admire. We, therefore, welcome the Pope's warning against "one-sided centralization by the public authorities," and his reliance upon "the initiative of individuals" and "free groups" and "local work centers."

Similarly, Pope Paul VI in *Populorum Progressio*, although wishing to supplement "the mere free play of competition," warns public authorities to "avoid the danger of complete collectivization or of arbitrary planning, which, by denying liberty, would prevent the exercise of the fundamental rights of the human person." And he describes those programs which should supplement the free play of competition as enabling each human being "to be the instrument of his own material betterment, of his own moral progress and of his spiritual growth." That is, each human being ought to be free, self-reliant, self-determining, even while cooperating with others politically, economically, culturally.

Between the individual and the centralized state, therefore, there is, in the words of Pope John Paul II:

> . . . a wide range of intermediate bodies with economic, social and cultural purposes. . . bodies enjoying real autonomy with regard to the public powers, pursuing their specific aims in honest collaboration with each other and in subordination to the demands of the common good. . . living communities both in form and in substance in the sense that the members of each body would be looked upon and treated as persons and encouraged to take an active part in the life of the body.

Only an open, free market allows such intermediate bodies economic breathing space; no command economy can cede them autonomy. Furthermore, the freedom of the market allows such bodies to *affect* the market, even to create new particular markets for new goods and services. Markets allow for foresight and providence on the part of individuals and associations.

We judge markets to be by far the most successful social device ever discovered for keeping the future open, for instituting needed initiatives, and for meeting unpredicted challenges with wit and invention. The human race has by now experienced many planned societies. "By their fruits, ye shall know them." (Matt. 7:20) From all the lessons of experience, we emphatically reject the illusion of rationalistic planning by experts, by states, or even by self-constituted planning groups.

By vivid contrast, we favor the virtues of providence, practiced by each individual, by associations of many sorts, and by the citizenry of entire communities. Taking thought for the future is a demanding exercise, which requires the talents and energies of all. By the principle of subsidiarity, they are most provident who best know the feel of concrete realities closest to them. "Strategic Planning" even within individual firms is often no match for swiftly changing economic realities, as recent evidence shows. Thus, those who try to make even tentative strategic judgments—whether in government, entire industries, local regions, individual firms, communities, or families— do well to consult as widely and as shrewdly as possible.

If the wealth hidden by the Creator in this largely untapped planet is to be brought forth in sufficient abundance to nourish the whole human family, today's choices must be made wisely, efficiently, creatively, flexibly. A dynamic world economy is essential to this task. Such dynamism exacts great spiritual costs. Change is at its heart; social inventiveness—provident, cooperative—must keep pace. The condition of inventiveness is liberty.

For this reason, we humbly propose as a motto for the church in this new age, not solely Justice and Peace, but Liberty, Justice, and Peace. The Liberty of voluntary cooperation. The Liberty of providence. Liberty under law, Liberty suffused with moral purpose. Liberty, in the end, is the contribution of the experience of the United States to the social teaching of the Catholic Church: LIBERTY AND JUSTICE FOR ALL.

The Two Catholic Letters on the U.S. Economy

MICHAEL NOVAK

NOW THAT THE FLURRY of early discussion has passed, it's time to evaluate the pastoral letter of the Catholic bishops on the U.S. economy more coolly, and with it the lay letter issued by thirty-one Catholic laypersons headed by William E. Simon.

The bishops' letter has four parts. First, the bishops give a sound justification for their concern about the effects of economic life on the religious life of persons and families.

Second, they give a biblical justification for Christian concern about the poor most of all.

Third, they set forth at some length a new interpretation of the last one hundred years of Catholic social thought, distilling it into several useful (but theologically debatable) guiding principles.

Finally, in the longest part of their letter, they select several specific areas and make quite specific recommendations on poverty and welfare, employment, cooperative social planning, and foreign aid. This last part, especially the short section on poverty, received most of the early public attention.

In some ways, the press may have been misled by the short press summary the bishops attached to their draft, which, much more than the draft itself, stressed highly political state-oriented analyses and state solutions.

The bishops are not alone in wanting to help the poor. Since 1962, when John F. Kennedy launched the extensive welfare reform that was to lead to "the Great Society," the people of the United States have become nearly thirty times more generous in governmental aid to the poor (cash and in-kind), on an annual basis. The problem is, the design of these expenditures seems to be causing extensive damage to poor families, as shown in startling figures

---

Michael Novak is a well-known Catholic layman and author who contributes regularly to several periodicals. Among his many books are *The Spirit of Democratic Capitalism* and *Freedom With Justice: Catholic Social Thought and Liberal Institutions.*

for illegitimacy, single-parent households, and the rapidly growing number of children affected thereby.

You don't have to be Catholic to wish to help the poor. John Stuart Mill observed a century ago that the measure of a good society is how well it helps its weakest members. But actually helping the poor is quite different from merely wanting to help. The argument today concerns the effectiveness of programs, not simply their good intentions. The ideas offered by the bishops are, mainly, old ideas, some of which have failed in the past. In principle, most Americans believe in helping the poor; in practice, many both left and right are uneasy about the methods so far used.

Insofar as the poor or the unemployed can be helped by jobs, economic activism is by far a better agent of change than political activism. The bishops recognize this. Yet they actually have very little advice for economic activists—workers, entrepreneurs, managers, finance officers, and the like. Their letter often approaches practical problems in the light of what the state can or should do. This is a disappointment.

The lay letter, issued just before the bishops' letter (and not in criticism of it, but as a complement) by William E. Simon, myself, and twenty-nine other Catholic laypersons, suggests that Catholic laypersons in suburban parishes, skilled in entrepreneurship, should be invited to put personal efforts into helping Catholics in poor parishes to teach such skills and help local economic activists get businesses started. In poor neighborhoods, there is invariably a lot of work to be done and a lot of unemployed labor—*some* catalyst is needed to put these two factors together creatively.

Taking a Stand on Specifics

The entire last part of the bishops' letter reads rather more like a party platform than does the parallel part in the lay letter. The lay group brought the argument down to specifics, and then mentioned a wide range of specific programs, but without endorsing any. The religious point is to show how the moral principles apply to concrete approaches, but without foreclosing the question about which specific approaches will actually work. Two persons sharing common moral ideals might well disagree about which practical courses of action will best achieve them. The bishops' draft took the risk of being more partisan.

In fact, U.S. Catholics include radicals and conservatives, moderates and liberals. All devout Catholics do not and need not agree on specific political programs.

As the press has widely noted, the bishops' document leans to the left of Mondale; *Newsweek* called it "God as Social Democrat." Is it right to divide the church along political lines? Should not the bishops stand above all factions? No moderate or conservative critic had a chance to read the bishops' draft before it appeared, in order to warn the bishops away from needlessly inflammatory language.

For example, the bishops use the slogan that Tom Hayden and Jane Fonda have chosen to describe their agenda: "economic democracy." They repeat the slogan of the sixties: "Participation in the decisions which shape our lives." The full implications of these slogans seem to escape the bishops; they voice none of the necessary criticisms.

Endorsing 'Economic Rights'

But the biggest bombshell in the bishops' letter has so far been overlooked. Several times the bishops call for new "economic rights" to go along with traditional U.S. political and civil rights. In stressing this point on television and in interviews, the bishops show that they are serious about this. At least one member of the bishops' writing staff has said they intend to inspire a "radical" restructuring of American society. The Jesuit who wrote the relevant sections, David Hollenbach, has even suggested: "The right to subsistence has never been a right protected by the Constitution, but the bishops are saying we need that basic right."

Such a move would surely alter the role of the state in the U.S. economy. For if the state is given the duty to supply every American with a job, income, and other benefits, the state will also gain immense new powers: to limit population for example, and to send people where the jobs are (Siberia!). In many states today, economic rights do not supplement, in practice they replace, the rights of individuals. Conflicts of rights are inevitable. Granting the state such new responsibilities and powers is no light step.

"Economic democracy" and "economic rights" go far beyond the ideal of helping the poor. They offer a rival design for the U.S. political economy. Indeed, many of us think, they are not compatible with it. One can, of course, speak of "the right to a job" merely in a declarative manner, not intending a fully formed constitutional right. In that case, the bishops do not really intend "radical restructuring."

Heavy debate is bound to continue during 1985. The bishops' second draft (due in May) and their third draft (due in November) are likely to be much improved.

A 'Radical' Dissent

ANDREW M. GREELEY

IS IT POSSIBLE, I wonder, to dissent from the chorus of praise for the bishops' pastoral on the economy and not be identified with the nervous neighings of such critics as neocapitalist Michael Novak? I hope it is, because I propose in this essay to dissent on two grounds, one that might be called "conservative" (though I would think of it as professional) and one that seems to me to be radical.

My first criticism is that the bishops have used the authority of religion, Scripture, and their office to settle complex, intricate, problematic, and ambiguous economic issues about which the even most skilled economists would hesitate. Moreover, in thus cutting the Gordian knot of economic uncertainty and complexity, the bishops do not often acknowledge that there is an opposite position that men and women of good mind and good will might embrace. Minimally, this failure makes their document sloppy. At worst it hints at intellectual dishonesty.

My second criticism is that the bishops, because of an amazing failure to understand the classical Catholic social theory of an organic society, do not offer strong enough criticism of the hyper-centralization of power in American capitalism or of the collective irresponsibility of corporate bureaucracies that results from that centralization.

As a result of this twin failure, the bishops, their staff, and their advisors have produced a document that is little more than a rehash of the party-line-liberal conventional wisdom of five to fifteen years ago, with a touch of class-conflict ideology (the poor against the powerful) that hints vaguely at pop-Marxism. They have, in other words, provided religious underpinning for the latter-day New Deal of the 1980 Democratic party platform. The pastoral adds virtually nothing new to the discussion of the American economy at a time when many of us who were committed to the New Deal find our-

Andrew M. Greeley, a priest of the Archdiocese of Chicago and a nationally known sociologist, journalist, and novelist, is also an associate of the National Opinion Research Center in Chicago. This article first appeared in the January 12, 1985, issue of *America* and is reprinted by permission of the author.

selves intrigued by the neo-liberal critique, a critique of which the pastoral seems singularly unaware. The bishops' recommendations for economic policy differ only marginally from suggestions one could have gleaned from the op-ed pages of liberal publications in the late 1970s and very early 1980s. The bishops, their staff, and their advisors have not done what was both possible and important: they have not contributed a special and uniquely Catholic perspective.

I will illustrate my first criticism with six instances, noting in advance that I do not necessarily embrace any of the positions that I cite the bishops as ignoring. In all the instances I find the evidence so gray and uncertain that I take my own position (for what little it might be worth) as a matter of instinct and not a matter of the religious certainty that the bishops manifest.

While they frequently admit the uncertainty of economic issues and reaffirm their pious intent not to pose as experts on these matters, they repeatedly make confident policy recommendations, about which most economists, even those supporting the recommendations, would be much less confident.

1. Speaking of tax reform, *the bishops insist on progressive tax rates as a matter of justice.* In the present context that seems to mean an endorsement of Senator Bill Bradley's (D.-N.J.) bill over Representative Jack Kemp's (R.-N.Y.). I wonder how the bishops can be so sure. The argument for the flat tax, and especially for Congressman Kemp's flat tax, is that progressive tax rates have created a situation in which the tax code has in fact become regressive and that a flat-rate reform will actually increase taxes on the rich because it will be the occasion for destroying the accumulated tax shelters of the ages. Moreover, it would be contended by supporters of the congressman's proposal, progressive rates will always produce such an effect.

My own instincts are with Senator Bradley's three rates; the senator is a Democrat; the congressman's wasp enthusiasm rubs me the wrong way; I did not like the American Football League; and the congressman's son presided over a defeat of my Chicago Bears this year. While the first reason is the main one, I cite the others because it seems to me that the bills are similar enough and the evidence so obscure that one can make a choice between two very similar measures only on instinctual grounds.

Which bill helps the poor more? How can anyone, even a bishop, be so certain as to provide moral and religious support for one and in effect denounce as immoral and irreligious the supporters of the other?

I also wonder what will happen when someone on the U.S. Catholic Con-

ference staff notices what the Bradley bill does to charitable contributions.
My bet is that the Catholic lobbyists will dash madly to Capitol Hill to pro-
test the 14 per cent exclusion for charitable contributions.

2. *The bishops call for a redistribution of wealth in America to curtail
if not eliminate poverty.* In their description of the extent of American poverty they use one set of statistics—the worse-case set—and do not acknowledge that there are other sets of statistics that would present a somewhat
different picture. They do not, for example, indicate how the proportion of
the population below the poverty line changes when one takes into account
"in-kind" payments through such measures as food stamps, Medicaid, and
housing subsidies. Ben Wattenberg, using census statistics, estimates that
when those payments are taken into account, the proportion of the population beneath the poverty level is between 8 and 9 per cent, 18 million people instead of the 38 million reported by the bishops (down from 22 per cent
in 1959).

The purpose of this observation is not to say that the 18 million figure is
acceptable or that Mr. Wattenberg's statistics are right and the bishops' are
wrong. They measure different things. Rather, my point is that by failing
to take into account the effect on the poverty population of in-kind payments
(not as good, I admit, as employment income but a lot better than nothing)
the bishops give a less than fully rounded portrait of American society. Either they know about the impact of in-kind payments and they do not mention it because if would weaken their rhetoric. Or they do not know about
them, and then someone—bishops or staff—has not done enough homework.
Mr. Wattenberg's work is not cited, and he is not listed among those who
gave testimony at the bishops' hearings.

Moreover, they do not admit that there is a serious and responsible economic opinion, subscribed to by many who oppose poverty as much as do
the bishops, that there are severe constraints on how much redistribution
can occur in any industrial society and that the Gini ratio (Corraco Gini's
measure of inequality) in the United States is relatively low (the lowest, the
last time I looked, was to be found in South Korea). It may be possible, in
this opinion, to force down the Gini ratio a few more points, but poverty
must be eliminated more by increasing the size of the economic pie than by
massive redistribution. My argument in this case is not that this position
is correct (candidly I don't know and I'm not sure anyone else does either),
but that it is a respectable and defensible position and ought not be thrown

out of court without a mention, especially since, if this school of thought is to be believed, attempts at redistribution will impede the increase of the economic pie.

3. *The bishops, their advisors, and their staff attribute much of the poverty in the United States to racial discrimination.* In fact, many students of the subject, including William Wilson, the black sociologist, now argue that discrimination is caused not by race but by social class and that all low-income groups, black, brown, and white, suffer a form of discrimination rooted mainly in their lack of educational success. Dr. Wilson's position (supported in part by elaborate mathematical models developed by Professor Michael Hout) may not be correct, but it is neither unreasonable, self-evidently wrong, nor absurd. Yet the bishops effectively dismiss it by not deeming it worthy of mention. Note that if Dr. Wilson is correct, the most important social-policy conclusion is not racial quotas or massive income transfers but herculean efforts to improve the quality of education available to the poor. The bishops et al. do not seem notably concerned by that sort of reform.

4. *The bishops unhesitatingly call for a greater transfer of funds to Third World countries,* a position that, on the face of it, seemed obviously Christian. Yet some students of the problem, including some economists in the less developed countries, think that most such transfers are not healthy and do more harm than good to the receiving nations. Others, more numerous and including some associated with the liberal Overseas Development Council, contend that a transfer of funds (with $15 billion a year as the upper limit of the contribution from the developed world that the less developed world could absorb) without agreement from the receiving nations about internal redistribution of wealth is fruitless. Consider, for example, that the massive transfer payments imposed by OPEC have not notably diminished poverty in Venezuela, Nigeria, or Mexico.

The matter is complex, obscure, difficult. But not for the bishops. They have simple, clear, and unequivocal answers to this very equivocal problem.

For obvious reasons, one supposes, they are silent on the population problem in the Third World. Yet that silence raises, does it not, some questions about the integrity of their compassion? They are virtually the only commentators on the problems of the poor countries who shy away from the population issue.

They are on much safer grounds when they call for the lowering of trade barriers as a means of correcting world poverty and inequality; but this recommendation creates another intractable problem to whose intractability the bishops do not attend.

5. *The hierarchy et al. want the United States, at the same time it lowers trade barriers, to diminish the level of structural or frictional unemployment.* They show no signs of comprehending that if you lower barriers, let us say, to Trinidadian steel and Brazilian automobiles, you will put workers in Port of Spain and São Paulo in direct competition with workers in South Chicago and Detroit. In any such competition the ineffecent American industries will suffer, and structural unemployment will increase. How do you balance these two highly desirable economic goals? No one knows for sure, but everyone who has thought about it, except apparently the bishops, their staff, and their advisors, realize that there are no easy answers and that the problem will be permanently intractable.

Unfortunately, the bishops did not bother to ask themselves what were the reasons for the lack of competitiveness of some American industries when confronted with foreign competition. What mistakes led to the situation in which, for example, Youngstown and Detroit will never be the same again because of failures of American steel and automotive production? If the bishops et al. had addressed this question, they might have been moved to understand better their own tradition of social criticism and see its implications for the hoary, muscle-bound, and inefficient heavy industries in this country.

6. Finally, *the bishops categorically endorse existing welfare programs and call for an increase in them,* with no hint that they are aware that many liberals and neo-liberals have lost confidence in the welfare approach to poverty. Need I say that this loss of confidence is not based on the assumption that society need do nothing about the poor? Rather, it is based on the growing conviction that most of what can broadly be called welfare, especially programs introduced since 1967, does not work and indeed does more harm than good. The pastoral cites Michael Harrington as one of those who offered testimony at their hearings. But there is no reference to Charles Murray, or any footnote citation to his *Losing Ground.* Yet Mr. Murray's argument—that antipoverty programs of the sort introduced since 1967 have caused pov-

erty rather than eliminated it—is important and not unpersuasive, even, for example, to the liberal (not neo-liberal) *New Republic.* How can the bishops et al. be so convinced that Charles Murray and those who have come to the same conclusions are so obviously wrong that their position need not even be mentioned?

If the bishops wish to take positions on highly contingent and problematic economic policy issues, would it not be more becoming for their opinions to be stated with a modesty and humility that indicated their awareness of the intractability of the problems about which they are talking? Ought they not be generous enough to admit that many issues are so complex that men and women of wisdom and integrity might well disagree with them?

But such modesty and humility and generosity are absent from the pastoral. The bishops take their stands with the same assertiveness with which in other contexts they denounce abortion and birth control. Thus they say that they "believe that an unemployment rate of 3 to 4 per cent is reasonable." Whence comes this faith? From a study of the economics of full employment? If so, why don't they describe their evidence and the arguments with which they refute those who might disagree?

Or from revelation or from a study of the Bible and the principles of social ethics? If so, are those who disagree so immoral that they can be dismissed without discussion?

One can never be sure whether the self-confident certainty of a particular policy recommendation is based on ethics or economics or a mixture of both or merely on the bishops' own pious hopes; one does not know whether one is dealing with divine faith, human faith, or mere opinion. All one can be sure about is that the bishops have simple and assertive answers to intricate and problematic issues, opinions, perhaps, but expressed in the categories of divine faith. In lesser men this absence of humility and generosity to adversaries would be called arrogance.

Other Weaknesses

In addition to the six samples cited above, I find a number of other weaknesses in the view of the bishops et al. of the American economy. They do not mention that America has created *27 million new jobs* in the last twenty years, something duplicated nowhere else in the world, even proportionately. This fact would suggest that for all its weaknesses the American economy still has the resources to produce jobs for its working force (which is not to say that it is excused from even more effort to search out the causes of unemployment and deal with them).

There is but one passing mention of *inflation* in the pastoral and no sense that the late 1970s inflation was a world disaster comparable to the Great Depression. One wonders how isolated religious leaders are from their people when they do not realize that much poverty and suffering were caused by the Ayatollah Khomeini/Jimmy Carter inflation and that all over the world people live in mortal terror of continued or increased inflation rates.

Moreover, they do not seem concerned by the impact on interest rates of the enormous *American budgetary deficit* and the results of these high rates on the Third World debt repayments, a problem to which they devote considerable attention. How can they not realize that a deficit of $200 billion a year, continuing indefinitely, constitutes a horrendous moral concern?

Finally, there is no mention of what may be the most widespread practice of injustice in our country: *the underground or cash economy.* It is not an unreasonable estimate that a quarter of the income in the United States is not reported and hence not taxed because those payments take place in cash transactions for which there are no records. Those of us whose income is all in checks (which I would suspect is true especially of the poor) thus have to pay not only our own tax bills but tax for that large portion of national income that is never declared. How can the bishops not tell their congregants to cut that out?

By way of summary, there are grave omissions in the episcopal analysis of the American economy, some of which might seem to those who take the opposite positions—while sharing the bishops' goals of the reduction of poverty—as irresponsible, if not intellectually dishonest.

The 'Organic Society'

My second objection is more radical, more fundamental, and, to be honest, more puzzled. The bishops, their staff, and their advisors seem unaware of the old Catholic tradition of the "organic society" and how that tradition demands a telling critique of the concentration of power in the American economy and the resulting irresponsibility of large corporate bureaucracies. How, I wonder, can this be?

I must pause to summarize briefly the "organic society" theory, because one can no longer assume that it is known even by readers educated in Catholic colleges. Broadly speaking, there are four contending social theories that

have been inherited from the late eighteenth century: capitalism and socialism believe in the centralization of power and decision-making and inatten-
tion to, if not outright opposition toward, the working in the economy of the
traditional social ties of family, friendship network, work group, local community, and such "nonrational" ties as religion and ethnic group. Anarchism
and Catholicism both rejected these two manifestations of bourgeois "liberalism" in favor of an economic order that is decentralized, pluralistic, and organic in the sense that it is tied in with and respectful of the most intimate
relationship networks of a person's life. Capitalism and socialism rejected
the "corporate" society of late feudalism. Catholicism and anarchism ad-
vocated in opposition a return to the freedoms and protections of that decentralized, pluralistic, and cooperative social order. (Obviously there was
nostalgia in this position, but the appeal of the nineteenth-century Catholic
and anarchist social thinkers—Proudhon, for example—was to the ideal of
the organic society as against the ideal of the bourgeois society.)

This Catholic theory was widely taught in seminaries and universities before 1960 and articulated by such writers as John Cronin, J. A. Messner,
John A. Ryan, Yves Simon, the younger Jacques Maritain, and Oswald von
Nell-Breuning (the author of the first draft of the encyclical *Quadragesimo
Anno*). It can be conveniently summarized under three principles—person-
alism, pluralism, and subsidiarity: (1) society exists for the good of the person and not vice versa; (2) that good is best served when power is held not
by one social institution (the state) but by a wide variety of overlapping and
crosscutting institutions; and (3), most important, the possession of power
ought to be decentralized as much as possible: nothing should be done by
a larger and higher organization that can be done as well by a lower and
smaller organization.

To put it in contemporary terms: The welfare of any society is measured
by its attitudes toward its microstructures. The more an institution puts
decision-making power into the microstructures, the healthier and the more
efficient such an institution will be.

As E. F. Schumacher (not cited by the bishops, by the way) argued on his
pilgrimage to the Catholic social theory and eventually to the Catholic
Church: "Small is beautiful." Or as I would rephrase it, nothing ought to
be bigger than is absolutely necessary.

The bishops do mention all three of these principles, but they do not seem
to understand either pluralism or subsidiarity, especially the latter, which
they see as applying only to the state (and which they cite, rather perversely
it seems to me, only as a justification of greater government intervention).

Hence, they are mute on the centralization of monopoly power in American industry, a problem that one can persuasively argue is at the root of all the other issues to which the bishops address themselves.

They do not seem to comprehend that their own social theory should compel them to question the humanity and the efficiency of all large corporate bureaucracies: governmental, educational, industrial, professional (including unions), military, and even ecclesiastical. Perhaps the pastoral does not challenge the power of vast corporate bureaucracies because it is itself a product of one such bureaucracy.

If, for example, one asks how American steel and automotive industries deterioriated from greatness to rustiness in the space of a decade or a decade-and-a-half (at the most), one is forced to respond that both industries had become overcentralized, bogged down in internal corporate struggles, shortsighted, unimaginative, and incapable of competition with foreign industries, precisely because they were bloated, muscle-bound, sluggish, oversized monopolies that for many years did not have to worry about price competition. Why modernize when you seem to control your own universe?

Or compare the friendliness, efficiency, and low costs of, let us say, People Express, with the unfriendliness, inefficiency, and high costs of any of the major American air lines. P.E. knows how to load a widebodied plane in a hurry and still be polite and courteous. United, for example, does not. The former is no bigger than necessary. The latter is much larger than needs be, and hence is almost by definition both incompetent and unfriendly.

I.B.M., because of its sheer size, reputation, and marketing muscle, has been able to interject itself into the personal computer market with equipment made from "off the shelf" components and become dominant despite the fact that its smaller competitors (especially Radio Shack and Apple) are thought by many of us who use personal computers to make better, cheaper, and more efficient products.

American antitrust laws are virtually inoperative. When they are enforced, as in the A.T.&T. case, the result is both higher prices and less efficient service for consumers. Small is beautiful and big is ugly, but big wins, not because it is better but because it is big.

The Cause of Structural Unemployment

The bishops et al. might dismiss these examples as irrelevant. What difference do airplane travel, personal computers, and telephone service make to the poor? In a society where sheer size makes inefficiency and irresponsibility both dominant and irrelevant, the poor suffer, not because they wish to fly or use a personal computer or make a long-distance call, but because structural unemployment is an inevitable result of the concentration of power and the inefficiency that such concentration causes. Both workers and consumers are powerless in the face of giants whose strength comes from size and not from effectiveness or responsibility.

The pastoral emphasizes jobs and income as preconditions for economic democracy. They are required certainly, but they do not suffice. In an economy dominated by lethargic and inefficient giants, even the employed and the non-poor have little economic power. More to the point, perhaps, they have no opportunity to contribute from their ingenuity and insight to a more efficient corporate enterprise that would, because of this contribution, create greater productivity and more jobs.

Anyone steeped in the theory of the organic society would react almost immediately to the centralization of power in the American society. Such an observer would suspect, almost a priori, that excessive size and unjustified concentration of power are its most fundamental weaknesses and the most serious cause of both poverty and unemployment. Moreover, a critic sensitized to the classic Catholic social theory would writhe in horror at the mergers, acquisitions, and corporation buyouts that have become a commonplace of American business life and that are devoid of social utility and contribute to an ever greater concentration of economic power and resultant inefficiency and inhumanity.

Recently in Chicago, two large food firms, Esmark and Beatrice, merged to form a super-large food firm. One heard nary a word of criticism from the Cardinal or peripatetic social activist Msgr. John Egan, who had protested vigorously against the threatened closing of the U.S. Steel South Works. Anyone aware of classic Catholic social theory would have instantly pointed out that the size and centralization of power of the new firm was an important part of the explanation for the decline of the American steel industry and would have asked what, in addition to profit for management and large stockholders, was the social justification for this increase of economic concentration.

Let me put it this way to Archbishop Weakland and his colleagues: Do you know what a leveraged buyout is? If you do, why did you not inveigh against the practice with all your oratorical powers? If you do not, why are you writing a pastoral on the economy? If your staff and advisors have not told you about it, why don't you get rid of them?

On Being 'Radical'

I have used the word "radical" in quotes in the title of this essay because, while I think the word is used appropriately of my critique of the pastoral, it is not the way the word is understood by Catholic peace-and-justice activists and staff members. To be "radical" in their sense of the word is to advocate greater state involvement and control of the economy; it marks your position as being closer to the socialism end of the capitalism/socialism continuum. By these standards the pastoral is not very radical, though one detects hints in the document of a lurking staff that would like to be far more explicitly "liberationist" in its orientation.

I feel that my critique of the pastoral is authentically radical, because I demand a more profound restructuring of American society. Instead of, or perhaps in addition to, advocating more money for existing government programs (about the effectiveness of many of which there is considerable doubt), the Catholic social theory of the organic society ought to have constrained the bishops to more fundamental challenges to the American economy.

A Catholic social perspective ought to suggest that the basic cause of unemployment is to be found in the hyper-concentration of power in mammoth industrial bureaucracies and that the root cause of poverty is the concentration of power in unresponsive educational bureaucracies. Moreover, the failures of both industrial and educational megaliths to respond to the causes of unemployment and poverty are aggravated by the even more massive federal megalith in which waste, mediocrity, unresponsiveness, and incompetence have reached dizzying heights of perfection.

How can anyone who has ever filled out a federal government form or tried to deal with the local Social Security office advocate more power and money to such agencies? Why do not the bishops also analyze the reasons that these agencies are so grossly incompetent and unresponsive? Why do they not offer recommendations for restructuring the functioning of such agencies in light of the principles of the organic society?

Unless the bishops are able to apply the principle of subsidiarity to all sectors of American society, their criticisms will be superficial and not radical enough. Unless the bishops are willing to reject the capitalism/socialism continuum as the only axis on which to view economic behavior, they will never do anything more than echo the fashionable liberalism of five years ago, whenever five years ago was. They will arrive on the scene, as always, a little breathless and a little late.

Ironically, Schumacher was only one of many social thinkers to articulate a Catholic social perspective in recent years while at the same time the church was abandoning its own unique approach to social problems. Sociologist James C. Coleman, for example, has recently predicted that concern for microstructures will mark the leading edge of social-policy progress in the remaining years of the century. Professor Coleman is especially concerned with the educational microstructure, which, as he has suggested to me in private conversations, is manifested quintessentially in the Catholic parochial school. Greeley's first law again: When others discover a Catholic insight, Catholics have just abandoned it.

Other Problems in the Pastoral

There are some other problems with the pastoral that require brief notice. Is it not hypocritical for an institution that usually pays its employees substandard wages, that frequently tries to prevent its own employees from organizing, and that systematically discriminates against women to denounce poverty, support unionization, and decry the feminization of poverty?

If I am told there is some self-criticism in the document, I must reply that I have too much respect for the episcopal ability to see the mote in the eye of others and ignore the beam in their own eye to think that such self-criticism will have any effect.

And is it not patronizing for bishops, all of whom live quite comfortably, to denounce their flocks for "consumerism"? I do not begrudge bishops freedom from economic worries (better a bishop who does not need money than one who does); yet might not their people be properly upset, when they must cope with inflation, higher taxes, education expenses, and health-care costs, to be told that their harsh consumerist acquisitiveness ought to be curtailed? Any serious sociology of this country—and the bishops' sociology is even less serious than their economics—would have to describe it at worst as a "post-consumerist" society.

Finally, was I the only one offended by Archbishop Weakland's television comment that Catholics probably did not accept the bishops' policy recommendations? How does he know that the ordinary Catholic is not as concerned about unemployment and poverty as he is? My data show that Catholics are if anything more concerned about these problems than are other Americans. If they are dubious about some of the hierarchy's policy recommendations, might it not be for the good reason that they believe, not without some reason, that these recommendations in great part support programs that have been already tried and found wanting? Whatever happened to the notion that the Holy Spirit can and does speak not only from the teaching church but also from the learning church? Does the archbishop believe that the magisterium (a name borrowed from eighteenth-century Lutheran theory, by the way) has a monopoly on truth, compassion, and social understanding?

Why the Pastoral Fails

Is there nothing good in the pastoral? Don't push me on it.

If it does not address the most fundamental problem of the American economy—concentration of power in ever more incompetent and unresponsive corporate bureaucracies, business, educational, and governmental—from the perspective of the classic Catholic social theory, it is a failure and nothing else needs to be said.

Whence this failure? At one level it may be the result of bad strategy in choosing one's perspective. The bishops tell us that their fundamental norm is whether a policy will help the poor. Beyond doubt, justice for the poor is the paramount issue. But it might not be wise to begin with that issue because such a beginning might lead to just what the pastoral produces: support for palliatives that deal with symptoms instead of criticism of fundamental weaknesses in the American corporate structure (which weaknesses, it must be noted, do not prove that there are any better societies in the world). I suspect that a strategy that began with the question of what is a healthy society and in what respect does American society depart from the model of health contained in the Catholic vision of the organic society would have produced more powerful responses to the question of what are the root causes of poverty and unemployment.

Furthermore, Marxism as well as capitalism has blinkers that prevent it from seeing the dangers in the excessively large institution in which too much power has been concentrated. As long as the giant institutions are controlled by the state (which for the Marxist means himself and his friends), Marxism has no problem with them. Indeed centralization of power for Marxism is not an evil but a positive good. The bishops denounce the giant multinationals—favorite targets for Catholic peace-and-justice protesters, not because they are too big but because the Third World states cannot control them. (Given the incompetency and corruption of many Third World governments, this might not be all bad.) Their failure to comprehend that the traditional Catholic social theory would be instantly suspicious that giantism is the cause of unemployment and other economic evils suggests that vague, pop-Marxist blinkers are operative among the bishops or more likely their staff. Note that I am not saying that vulgar Marxism may have made the pastoral too radical. I am saying rather that it may have prevented the pastoral from being radical enough.

Moreover, the bishops have every reason to be content with the product of their efforts. It has won them favorable media coverage and earned back some of the prestige they lost because of their failures as teachers of sexual ethics. Whether a pastoral is serious and profound is of less importance in such a game than whether it is well received in the liberal national media.

Their activist staff and advisors can also be pleased with the outcome. When they go to conferences, make presentations, or take stands (for these are the things that activists do), they will be hailed by their counterparts for their "liberalism," which means, of course, for their support of the liberal programs of a half-decade or more ago.

There is much self-congratulation among the bishops et al. over the long months of hearings and the hard work that went into the preparation of the pastoral. Actually, a glance at the footnotes and at the list of those who have testified reveals that the documentation for the pastoral is shockingly thin. A pastoral that would critique the violations of subsidiarity in every sector of American society from the perspective of the Catholic vision of the organic society would require at least five years of work. Who has time for that sort of thing? Certainly not the Catholic universities, where this study of the Catholic social ethic should have been taking place for the last two decades.

However, I think that the basic reason for the failure of the pastoral is that neither the bishops nor their staff are aware of the theory of the organic society. Their failure as proponents of the Catholic social theory comes from the fact that they do not know the theory. In the few discussions I have had with the peace-and-justice crowd, they seem not to understand subsidiarity at all. The organic society and the tradition that produced it as a vision antedates 1963, which is to Catholic thought what Planck's wall is to theoretical physics: the boundary of an era in which nothing fits our current assumptions. Neither malice nor trickery nor even incompetence explains the failure of the pastoral to root itself in the Catholic social tradition. Only ignorance of that tradition.

A Challenge to Readers

Let me present a challenge, not to the bishops et al. whom I cannot challenge, but to readers of replies to this critique of the pastoral. Assume that all replies will be patronizing, name-calling, motive-questioning documents. Also assume that they will try to pull sentences and paragraphs out of context to prove that the bishops et al. have really done what I say they have not done. Ignore all of that. Demand before you take a response seriously that it (a) articulate the theory of the organic society, (b) explain why that theory was not used to critique the concentration of power in unresponsive and inhuman corporate bureaucracies in all sectors of American life, and (c) describe what the bishops et al. propose to do about rewriting their pastoral to concentrate on the reconstruction of microstructures within and over against the musclebound megaliths that are the institutional causes of poverty and unemployment.

Till that unlikely response, I am forced to conclude, noisily *extra chorum,* that the pastoral is an inept and inadequate document, sometimes appearing to be short on intellectual honesty, occasionally smelling slightly of hypocrisy, almost always dealing with symptoms instead of root causes, almost never providing a uniquely Catholic contribution, and instead of too radical, not in fact radical enough.

Not radical enough because not Catholic enough.

Perils of the Prophet Motive

CHARLES KRAUTHAMMER

HAVING PRONOUNCED on the beginning of life (birth control and abortion) and on the end of life (nuclear weapons), America's Catholic bishops have now turned their attention to life's middle. The subject of their most recent pastoral letter is economics. More specifically, as a committee of lay Catholics (chaired by William Simon and Michael Novak) makes plain in a challenging dissent to the bishops, the subject is capitalism.

The first thing to strike an outsider about this intra-Catholic debate is the language. It takes time before one realizes that "co-creation" is a theological synonym for production (capitalism being, I suppose, the system of private ownership of the means of co-creation). It seems odd to find the Incarnation invoked to shore up the case for federalism. Or to hear one side of a debate on economics talk of the "true sanctity" of "discipleship in the midst of work," and the other to venture the view that "the gate to creativity is narrow and the way straight."

Of course, this is not the first time that an argument about capitalism has been couched in esoteric language. Its original critic (and coiner of the term) embedded his prose in an equally thick fog of German Idealism. But in the end we all learned to translate Marx.

With a similar act of translation, the crux of the disagreement between the bishops and the lay committee becomes clear. It is not quite that one side condemns capitalism while the other celebrates it, although that is the tone of the documents. It is more that the bishops are concerned with the failings of capitalism, and the lay committee with its successes. Given capitalism's historical record, it is not surprising that the laity have the better of it. One need not belabor the point. Few systems of political economy have been able to feed the vast majority of their people or give them liberty. Democratic capitalism has done both. Even according to the bishops' nar-

Charles Krauthammer is a senior editor of the *New Republic,* and this essay is reprinted by permission from the December 24, 1984, issue of that journal (© 1984, The New Republic, Inc.).

·row criterion for judging all economic institutions—"the preferential option for the poor"—democratic capitalism has been uniquely successful.

But beyond accounting for capitalism's achievements, the lay letter delicately assigns to any Catholic critique of capitalism a historical, and therefore an ironic, context. After all, the Catholic Church is one of those "privileged concentrations of power, wealth, and income" of which the bishops' letter takes such a dim view. The American church in particular has achieved that position of wealth and power thanks to the surpluses generated by capitalism, and the liberty to dispose of those surpluses which democratic capitalism bestows on citizens. Moreover, Catholicism's historical record as a frame for economic development is not particularly encouraging. One has only to compare Protestant North America to Catholic South and Central America, or Quebec (before it declericalized itself in the 1960s) to the rest of Canada, to make the point gently. No one has yet accused the Catholic ethic of being a source of economic dynamism.

The Absence of Humility

This is not, of course, to say that Catholicism stands refuted. Religion has other purposes. But it is to say that if a religious hierarchy decides to *make* one of its purposes a prescriptive analysis of how society is to produce and distribute wealth, that hierarchy, mindful of its own history, might proceed with a touch of humility. That quality is difficult to find in the bishops' letter.

Still, the absence of humility would hardly be an issue had the bishops simply delivered a prophetic message about society's responsibility for the widow and the orphan. Isaiah was not a retiring man. A contemporary reiteration of his message, while not particularly novel, would be important, especially in a political economy founded on the principle of self-interest. But in this age of Poland, Chile, and liberation theology—an age in which the church is making history throughout much of the world—the American bishops seem not content with prophecy. They insist on advocacy. They want the word made (or at least given) flesh. Hence the principal undertaking of the bishops' letter: to suggest how prophetic concern for the poor is to be put into practice in a modern industrial economy.

Now, prophets have a certain claim to arrogance. But when the prophetic message is accompanied by a social-science analysis and a social program, one should take care that the tone of magisterial righteousness not envelop the entire enterprise. The bishops let that tone trickle down to the most contingent, debatable assertion. Moral philosophy and economic analysis entail radically different epistemologies. One would hardly know it from reading this document.

Enough about tone. What about content? Grant that the bishops refuse to yield the miter when they don economic hats. Thus doubly outfitted, do they have anything to say?

The bishops' mission is not merely to identify the failures of capitalism—unemployment, poverty, homelessness—but to diagnose them. The diagnosis suffers from two shortcomings. First and most obviously, their vision is narrowed by a routine acceptance of liberal assumptions about the causes of social problems. For example, they declare current rates of unemployment "morally unjustified," particularly when compared to the 3 or 4 per cent that used to prevail at the peak of the business cycle. They discount the possibility that structural changes in the economy, rather than illiberal political choices, may have raised the level of "frictional" unemployment. Among the recent phenomena that might have contributed to this new condition, morally unjustified or not, are the expansion of the labor force with the influx of women; the constraining effect of the safety net—from Social Security to union rules to health and safety regulations—on capitalism's dynamism (and cruelty); and the vast dislocations in Western economies caused by OPEC's excise tax on energy. Which of these do the bishops propose to roll back?

Similarly, in discussing poverty, they note its "feminization," but so scrupulous are they to avoid any hint of blaming the victim that they avoid the question of whether unwed mothers and absent fathers bear some responsibility for their poverty and that of their children. The cause of underclass misery is located variously in sexism, racism, lack of child care—all the usual liberal suspects, save inadequate birth control.

The Bishops' Naïveté

But the poverty of the bishops' analysis derives from more than mere narrowness of vision. It is due most of all to a profound naïveté. And naïveté of a particular kind: a belief in the power of good intentions, and an accompanying obliviousness to the intractability of certain problems, particularly problems that arise from the conflict of competing societal goods.

Consider the plight of the homeless. The bishops ascribe this problem (and poverty and unemployment) to a lack of political will and a lack of an adequate theoretical framework. Any solution, they write, "must begin with the formation of a new cultural consensus that *all persons really do have rights in the economic sphere."* (Emphasis bishops'.) Must it? People are not sleeping in doorways because "economic rights," unlike political rights, "do not hold [a] privileged position in the cultural and legal traditions of our nation." In fact, twenty-five years ago economic rights were, if anything, less enshrined than today, and there were no armies of grate-dwellers. There are today, largely as a result of one of the finest reformist impulses of the Kennedy years, the freeing of the mentally ill from the snakepits to which they had been consigned for a century. It was decided to restore liberty to these people. But with liberty necessarily comes a diminution of security. We have an epidemic of homelessness today, not because we have yet to accept U.N. declarations on economic rights, but because of a perennial conflict between liberty and security, a conflict most acutely manifest in those people most vulnerable to the ravages of freedom. We can do more for the homeless by forcing them into shelters. We might do still more by forcing them back into institutions. Which shall it be? Perhaps in our reforming zeal we have chosen badly for these people. But choose we must. Even bishops have to choose.

The homeless are the extreme case. But they highlight a chronic dilemma that government faces when trying to help the powerless and the weak. With protection comes dependence. With liberty comes the prospect of failure and, for those who fail, misery. That's the central problem of all welfare policy. If you give money to someone conditioned on his inability to make money on his own, you have created a disincentive to work. And when he begins to work and you at some point cut off his welfare (as you must, or else you are being unfair to other low-paid workers who have never laid claim to welfare), you have created more disincentive. It simply won't do imperiously to proclaim that welfare programs "should encourage rather than penalize gainful employment." Of course they should. But exactly how?

Perhaps there was a time when paradox could be defeated by proclamation. But this is not the age of miracles. And even if it were, an economic document is hardly the place to demand them. The bishops are not daunted: "Efforts to generate employment," they declare, "should be aimed specifically at bringing marginalized persons into the labor force; should give priority to long-term jobs; should produce goods and services needed by society; should be as economically efficient as possible; and should include both the private and public sectors." That would be nice, wouldn't it? In a helpful expansion they urge that "employment programs that generate jobs efficiently without entailing large expense and increased inflation should be empha-sized." Another paradox, this time a Keynesian one, is banished. Why, even Jesse Helms would welcome a noninflationary employment policy. The interesting question, to use scientific parlance, is exactly what that policy would be.

Offering More of the Same

The bishops' nontautological remedies are only slightly less disappoint-ing. They amount to more Great Society programs, more foreign aid, and a hint of planning. Where have they been for twenty-five years? We now have a generation of experience with liberal social programs, and the bishops ap-pear to have just discovered them. Not that social generosity has been a fail-ure. Far from it. Its successes are many and of great significance. But the crisis of liberalism—and the consequent search for "new ideas"—comes from the realization that these remedies have reached the limits of their success. The structurally unemployed, the female-headed household, the homeless, the mentally ill—the very kinds of misery that concern the bishops—represent precisely those categories of chronic dependency that have proved resistant to Great Society cures. These are the residue cases. More of the same is not a program that offers much hope.

This is all the more true for the poor of the Third World. Even among the most internationally minded, the zeal for charitable handouts, for the soft-loan window at the World Bank, has waned. Experience has been cruel and unequivocal. Ten years ago, to argue that foreign aid was actually retard-ing development in many Third World countries was eccentric. Today, even at the height of the sub-Saharan famine, one finds such views on the front page of the *New York Times*.

Hunger in the world is not caused by "extractive" Western (or multina-tional) economic policies. And it will be improved only marginally by more positive assistance from the West. The bishops are surely right that such as-sistance remains a moral imperative: marginal improvement translates into many starving people saved. But they are wrong to imagine that it will have the slightest effect on the gap between rich and poor nations which they find so disturbing. (The problem, of course, is not the gap. If it were, that would quickly be solved by impoverishing the West—a perhaps unintended side-effect of the new international economic order the bishops seem to favor. The real problem is how to lift the Ethiopias of the world out of poverty.)

These countries are economic disaster areas primarily because of the actions of their elites: destroying indigenous food production with collectivization plans and low food prices designed to serve the city at the expense of the country (e.g., Tanzania); favoring white-elephant prestige projects, often undertaken with Western aid; and importing cheap (sometimes free) foreign food that undercuts local farmers. South Africa and Zimbabwe have escaped famine not because white managers are smarter, and not because rain falls preferentially on capitalist economies, but because economies subject to market discipline are self-corrective in a way that command economies can never be.

The experience of the West, and now of East Asia as well, suggests that capitalism is the most likely route to rapid development, and thus ultimately, if inconveniently, is *the* preferential option for the poor. But these are hardly lessons the bishops wish to learn. Capitalism, after all, is a system based on the vice of acquisitiveness. The bishops prefer to appeal to higher instincts, the spirit of "discipleship," the more selfless inclinations of man. This is an excellent basis for a sermon, but not a prudent principle on which to build an economy.

It is one thing for religious leaders to remind their politicians and parishioners of the prophetic duty to care for the poor. It is another thing when these prophets, armed with the authority of technical experts, produce an outline of exactly how that is to be undertaken in a complex political system. It is even worse when this analysis produces a call for repeal of the paradoxes of economic life, and for enactment of a spent political agenda. To have discovered liberalism and to have rediscovered the poor is perhaps an achievement for any ecclesiastical hierarchy. But it is no great contribution to American political discourse.

Can the Bishops
Help the Poor?

PETER L. BERGER

O N NOVEMBER 11, 1984, a committee of the National Conference of
Catholic Bishops, headed by Archbishop Rembert Weakland of Milwaukee, issued the first draft of a "Pastoral Letter on Catholic Social Teaching
and the U.S. Economy." Publication of the document had been carefully timed
for after the elections, to avoid the impression of political partisanship. Given
the contents of the draft, one can appreciate both the civic prudence of the
bishops and the annoyance of some Democratic-party politicians who, it was
reported, regarded it as less than helpful to have been assaulted repeatedly
during the campaign by Catholic bishops opposing abortion while this document, which would have given support to important portions of the Mondale/
Ferraro platform, was held back until after the Reagan landslide.

But the muses of symmetry were not asleep. For on election day itself an-
other document was issued, on the same topic, by a self-constituted Lay Com-
mission on Catholic Social Teaching and the U.S. Economy, headed by
William E. Simon and Michael Novak. Titled *Toward the Future: Catholic
Social Thought and the U.S. Economy,* it is, fairly enough, a document the
Republicans would have loved to have had at hand during the campaign.

The parallel character of the two documents is not accidental. The Lay
Commission, knowing what its bishops had been up to, was engaging in a
bit of preemptive damage control. Yet while the two documents came out
at the same time, and deal with the same subject matter, in one important
respect they are not comparable at all. The Simon/Novak report is the result of an unofficial lay initiative; it has no actual or potential standing in
terms of official church teaching. The pastoral letter of the Weakland committee, on the other hand, was commissioned three years ago by the assem-

Peter L. Berger is a professor of sociology at Boston University and the author of
many books. This article is reprinted by his permission from the February 1985 issue
of *Commentary.*

bled Catholic bishops of the United States. It is now to be discussed and revised, with a final version to be voted on by all the bishops in November 1985. At that point, the document will constitute official Catholic teaching—not, to be sure, on the level of an infallible pronouncement on faith and morality, but as an expression of the magisterial authority of the American episcopate, and as such to be taken very seriously by all Catholics.

This difference between the two documents is very significant. Because of it, and despite the fact that the Simon/Novak report is far superior both in its level of economic understanding and in the quality of its moral judgment, I will discuss the bishops' pastoral letter here in much greater detail. For what the Catholic bishops of the United States have to say is of greater import than a statement, no matter how sensible, of a group of Catholic laymen.

The bishops, however, say they have spoken out not merely to give moral guidance to Catholics but also to join their voice to the public debate. Addressing all Americans, they explicitly mention and invite comment from non-Catholic Christians and Jews, with whom they share a common biblical heritage. The remarks that follow, then, are a response by a non-Catholic Christian to this invitation.

The bishops' draft letter is organized into two major sections. The first deals with the theological and ethical presuppositions of their approach to economic life. The second draws specific applications to policy, with particular attention to the areas of employment, poverty, food and agriculture (not in the present draft but to be added), policies of economic collaboration, and relations between the United States and the world economy.

Stressing 'Communitarianism'

Few readers, Christian or Jewish, are likely to quarrel with the bishops' basic presupposition, namely, that "the dignity of the human person, realized in community with others," should be the fundamental moral criterion of economic life. Indeed, the Simon/Novak report, using almost identical language and citing the same authorities, also calls the dignity of the human person "the first principle of Catholic social thought."

As the bishops develop this proposition, however, one is struck by the emphasis they place on what they themselves call the "communitarian" character of the Christian vision of economic life. To be human, they write, is to hear "the call to community"; they tell us that "the goods of this earth are common property"; they cite Clement of Alexandria on the "communality of possessions"; they refer to "communal solidarity" and the "fullness of community." And they counterpose all this stress on communitarianism to something they deplore, the "selfish appropriation and exploitation" of the goods and resources of the world.

Now, the bishops are careful to say that they are not against private property as such, and one may surmise that they are also not necessarily against capitalism—though, very curiously, they avoid using the word throughout the document. Yet from the beginning a suggestion has been planted that there is something basically wrong with *our* economic arrangements—since, obviously, they are not communitarian. In making this suggestion, to be sure, the bishops stand in a long Catholic tradition of suspicion toward capitalism and all its works (a tradition, incidentally, that long antedates modern socialism). It is a tradition, as we shall see, that is openly challenged by the Simon/Novak document, which in this respect, at least, is a far more radical statement than the bishops'.

Aside from their emphasis on communitarianism, the bishops also tell us, reasonably enough, that the Christian approach to economic life must be informed by the "primacy of justice" and by an awareness of the "dangers of wealth." Then they go on to embrace the so-called "preferential option for the poor." This awkward phrase, proclaimed as church teaching at the 1979 meeting of the Latin American episcopate in Puebla, Mexico, encapsulates one of the leading ideas of liberation theology. It means, quite simply, that the criterion for judging the moral worth of a society is the fate of that society's poor. It also means (in the words of the bishops) that the church has a "prophetic mandate to speak for those who have no one to speak for them." Deriving from this "option for the poor" are "basic economic rights" which every society ought to guarantee to all its members.

A Preference for State Action

Shorn of its Guevarist undertones, the "preferential option for the poor" is an idea unlikely to shock many Jews or Christians. After all, it was Dr. Johnson, not exactly a theologian of liberation, who insisted that "a decent provision for the poor is the true test of civilization." But the rest of the bishops' argument here is shaky. A common assumption of democracy is that no one has a "mandate" (prophetic or otherwise) to speak for people who have not elected him as their spokesman; the Catholic bishops of the

United States have not been elected by any constituency of poor people. More importantly, even if there is something that could be called economic rights, just who or what is the society that is supposed to insure them? The bishops repeatedly disclaim a statist approach to economic life, yet when they come to specifics it is mainly state action that they recommend.

This, indeed, is one of the major substantive flaws of the pastoral letter. When the bishops refer to the fact that most American Catholics were once poor, they do so in order to criticize them for the temptation, in their new-found affluence, to be indifferent to the fate of today's poor. It does not occur to the bishops to ask how so many poor Catholic immigrants managed to achieve affluence within one or two generations in America. But if they had inquired into this tale of rags-to-riches, they would have discovered that it had very little to do with state actions or government policies; what it had a lot to do with was capitalism.

In view of the spirit animating the bishops' document, it is not surprising that, in dealing with the putative shortcomings of the American economy, they should zero in on inequalities of wealth and income. The bishops are careful to say that the ideal of distributive justice cannot be reduced to a simple arithmetical formula and that a certain degree of inequality can "sometimes" be justified. However, present levels of inequality, both in this country and among the nations of the world, they deem "morally unacceptable." (They make special mention of inequalities based on race and sex.)

Measures of income and wealth distribution are of course enormously complicated, but is it so clear that American society, as the bishops claim, exhibits a degree of inequality high enough to be labeled "morally unacceptable"? The driving forces in this area have considerably less to do with the political organization of a particular economy than with its location along a trajectory of industrial growth; when one compares capitalist with socialist economies at similar stages of industrial development, they evince surprisingly similar patterns of income distribution. Moreover, *all* industrial and industrializing societies show patterns of inequality that, to a large extent, resist political intervention. By what criterion is inequality to be deemed "sometimes" acceptable, sometimes not? Rather than fixing on the elusive ideal of "equality," those with a professed concern for the poor might consider absolute rather than relative standards of living. If such a criterion were applied to American society (and indeed to the other societies of industrial capitalism), the level of "moral acceptability" would surely rank among the highest in human history.

Domestic Policy Recommendations

So much for the bishops' diagnosis of the domestic scene. Their policy recommendations present rather a mixed bag. They call for a commitment to "full employment," which, following current convention, is defined as 3–4 per cent unemployment. By contrast, a level of 6–7 per cent unemployment is termed, again, "unacceptable," although we are not told by what superior moral insight the bishops find themselves able to accept the former but bound to condemn (prophetically?) the latter. To deal with poverty, or the "glaring disparities of wealth and income," they recommend tax reform; self-help programs among the poor to be stimulated by government; affirmative action, "judiciously administered"; improved child-care services; something that sounds like comparable worth ("persons who make comparable contributions to society are entitled to comparable rewards"); and welfare reform (for example, by legislating national eligibility standards and by removing provisions that penalize employment).

Different readers will find different items here on which to agree or disagree with the bishops. Some of their recommendations are quite sensible, although one must wonder why the authority of Catholic moral teaching has to be invoked to support, say, job-training programs. As for the overall strategy for dealing with the social and economic problems of America, it is Left-of-Center, corresponding remarkably with the agenda proposed by the Democratic party platform of 1984. And, like that platform, it can be described as modeled on an essentially European vision of social democracy.

I do not wish to be misunderstood on this point. The bishops do explicitly repudiate a collectivist ethic of economic life, and in this their document compares favorably with the 1983 statement by the Catholic bishops of Canada, which was indeed a massive attack on capitalism and, at least implicitly, an endorsement of socialism. One should be grateful for small favors: far better an American Catholic document that reads like a translation from Swedish than from Albanian. Yet it is ironic that the Catholic episcopate of the United States, feeling fully a part of American society and no longer constrained by the formerly marginal position of Catholics in that society, should find so little to learn from the American experience. In this, once again, the Simon/Novak document shows much greater ingenuity.

When we come to the area of economic relations between the United States and the Third World, the predispositions of the bishops become if anything easier to pinpoint. The footnotes refer us to Mahbub ul Haq, Jan Tinbergen, Barbara Ward, and, prominently, to the report of the Brandt Commission—all well-known sources for the view that the economic distress of the Third World is attributable to an "unjust international economic order." On the role of the multinationals in the Third World, there are references to the publications of the United Nations Center on Transnational Corporations, which are animated by a strong antagonism to capitalism, and to the 1974 book by Ronald Müller and Richard J. Barnet, *Global Reach,* which has become a basic source of anti-multinational propaganda. There are on the other hand no references to the work of Raymond Vernon, the most balanced analyst of this matter, and none to such pro-capitalist authors as P. T. Bauer and Melvyn Krauss. Thus, simply by consulting the sources relied upon by the bishops, one can pretty much predict what in fact the document delivers—a moderate (as opposed to radical) version of *tercermundismo,* or Third Worldism (to use the term coined, pejoratively, by the Venezuelan writer Carlos Rangel).

Morally this perspective may be inspired by a genuine concern for the poor, but empirically it is informed by a number of dubious assumptions. Foremost among these is the idea that much if not all of Third World poverty is due to dependency on the rich nations. In fact, however, as Bauer and others have pointed out, there appears to be, if anything, a *reverse* relation between poverty and dependency in Third World countries. Another false assumption of the bishops, implicit rather than explicit, has to do with their notion of the relevant parties to economic development. Thus, in their list of "actors" in international economic relations they mention nation-states, multilateral institutions (such as the World Bank), and multinational corporations; they completely omit the most important actors—individuals and businesses engaged in enterprise within Third World economies. That omission, more perhaps than anything else, reveals the flawed optics of the bishops' analysis.

The specific criticisms and recommendations of the bishops follow logically from their underlying assumptions. We are told that there must be "basic reform" in the international economic system, a "fundamental recasting, not simply a modification, of the present system." What they have in mind, alas, is something along the lines of the "New International Economic Order," a project whose guiding premise is that Third World governments represent the Third World poor, and are truly interested in alleviating their condition. There are, to be sure, instances in which this premise holds; but there are at least as many, if not more, in which it does not. In such cases, economic development, if it is to take place at all, will do so in spite of or even against the policies of the government. A "fundamental recasting" of the world economy in the form the bishops propose would only make development more difficult.

Along the same lines, the bishops want discussions between richer and poorer nations, aimed at a reform of the world economy. Here too they embrace a favorite item in the Third World agenda, that of a "North/South dialogue" (also called "global negotiations"). By definition, such a dialogue must take place among governments—including governments whose economic and other policies are inimical to development and thereby antagonistic to the interests of the poor in their own countries.

A similar point can be made about the priority the bishops would give in the Third World to the "basic human needs of the poor." This sounds unobjectionable, but the term "basic needs" is not innocent. It implies a particular strategy, one emphasizing immediate redistribution as against long-term economic growth; this is a strategy that carries with it great risks and human costs, and that is by no means self-evidently worthy of being singled out for favored moral distinction. Indeed, the "basic-needs" approach has been sharply criticized in the Third World itself, where it has been characterized as a paternalistic device for giving "welfare" without inquiring as to how underlying economic structures can in fact be permanently improved.

U.S. Policy Toward the Third World

What policies, then, should the United States adopt toward the Third World? According to the bishops, the United States (or, more precisely, the Reagan administration) views the Third World too much through the prism of "East/West" relations. But if so, this is due not to some perverse myopia but to the facts of energetic Soviet expansion throughout the Third World. The United States, say the bishops, gives too much military aid as compared with other forms. Again, is this traceable to moral perversity or is it a response to events on the international scene that are not of American making? The United States, the litany proceeds, favors bilateral aid when what is needed is aid through multilateral institutions. But experience has shown that bilateral programs are more easily monitored in terms of results, and less likely to be absorbed into the cesspool of corruption all too often characterizing Third World political structures. The United States is accused by the bishops of giving too little aid as a percentage of gross national product. This assumes that the more aid, the more development—a very questionable assumption indeed; it also assumes, no less dubiously, that government aid is more beneficent than the activities of private business.

To replace current policies, the bishops also make a number of specific recommendations, none of real merit. There should be an international equivalent of affirmative action: in view of the less than spectacular success of these policies in improving the condition of their intended beneficiaries domestically, the bishops' faith in their efficacy on the international level seems a little misplaced. There should be less military aid and fewer arms sales: a *pium desideratum,* to be sure, but addressed with at least equal propriety to the Kremlin, Colonel Qaddafi, and the Palestine Liberation Organization (to mention but a few of the "actors" whose collaboration on this agenda would have to be secured). The United States should devise more favorable trade arrangements with Third World countries: definitely, but any such trade benefits to the Third World would be in tension not only with the goal of full employment for Americans that the bishops endorse but with their demand for a turning-away from "consumerism." Some Third World debts should be forgiven: perhaps, but what would this do to the future credit needs of Third World governments? The United States should give more aid, especially through the International Development Association: doubtful. Private investment in Third World countries should be "appropriate" to their economies: probably so, but who is to make such judgments?

Not all the bishops' criticisms of current American policies in the Third World are misplaced; most are. Not all the bishops' positive recommendations are bad; most are. The problems of underdevelopment will not be solved by international agreements among governments, useful though some of these may be. Nor can development be fostered primarily by state actions on either the national or the international level. The principal "actors" in the drama of development are people engaged, alone or in conjunction with others, in economically productive enterprises. There *are* cases of successful development in what only a few years ago were very poor countries—such as South Korea or Taiwan. And there are lessons to be drawn from the experience of these countries. But the bishops are in a very bad position to learn them. For, as in the case of their approach to poor American Catholics who have attained affluence, they never ask the most important question: just *how* does a society move from poverty to affluence?

It is this question, by contrast, that most interests the Lay Commission. Its report, of course, appeals to the same Catholic social teachings as do the bishops, citing the same papal encyclicals and invoking the same basic principles: human dignity, the social nature of man, social justice. But the report also finds that the American political economy embodies a number of moral principles that Catholics ought to approve of: free association, cooperation, and "self-interest, rightly understood." All this is related by the Lay Commission to the Christian notion of "co-creation": human beings, in their activity, "following the clues left by God."

Thus there is, according to Simon and Novak, an "innate virtue" to enterprise. They are careful not to leave the impression that they endorse every aspect of capitalism in practice, or that they oppose government action to remedy particular social ills. But they do point to two linkages that the bishops totally ignore—that between capitalism and democracy, and that between capitalism and successful economic development. They assert these connections not on grounds of doctrine, but on the basis of readily available empirical evidence: there is not a single democracy in the world that is not part of the capitalist world economy, and there is not a single non-capitalist case of successful economic development in the Third World. Thus, precisely on the grounds of the "preferential option for the poor," Simon and Novak came out on the side of capitalism.

Although some of their specific recommendations are not too different from those of the bishops—for example, on employment-generation, or on the question of free trade—the whole tone of the Simon/Novak document is very different. Where the bishops mainly criticize America, while allowing that it deserves some praise, the Lay Commission mainly praises America, while conceding that there is room for criticism and improvement. In this difference, it is fair to say, the two documents faithfully reflect the two political parties in the country today.

Endangering Catholicity

Well, one might ask, what is the harm in that? By way of an answer, imagine for a moment that the bishops had issued the document signed by Simon and Novak. If so, they would certainly have earned a higher grade in economic and political competence; but would we really want them to be blessing American capitalism and its works, any more than we would want them to denigrate them? What, in that event, about Catholics who happen to believe that American capitalism *is* "morally unacceptable"? Should they be read out of the community of faith? These questions touch on a vital theological issue, the manner in which social and political partisanship endangers one of the essential *notae ecclesiae,* or "marks of the church": namely, its catholicity.

The bishops claim that the application of their ethical presuppositions and their method of reasoning to the subject at hand constitutes a major contribution, for both Catholics and non-Catholics. But Simon and Novak, drawing on the same ethical presuppositions and the same method of reasoning, have come to very different conclusions. The fact that Catholic moral teaching is so flexible as to lend legitimacy to such opposed perspectives on reality raises serious questions about the alleged contribution of this method of moral reasoning. Both major political camps find it amenable to their views. The pity is that the official church, which has better things to do, should be lining up on one side.

In both the present document and in their 1983 pastoral letter on war and peace, the Catholic bishops are increasingly sounding like the left wing of the Democratic party gathered for prayer. From one perspective, I suppose, this development could be seen as a step in the "indigenization" of American Catholicism. But not quite in the way envisaged by the bishops. For in their political and ideological positioning, the Catholic bishops are following in the well-worn footsteps of a major segment of official mainline Protestantism. If their pastoral letter reads in places like a translation from the Swedish, it is also, minus a few papal quotations, reminiscent of the social-action pronouncements of the United Methodist Church. This, given the fact that what we are supposed to have here at last is the voice of a Catholic community fully at home in America, is to my mind profoundly sad.

Rejecting the Role of Mediator

There is here, finally, a great missed opportunity. If any role in the social and political arena is natural for official spokesmen of religion, it is the role of mediators. For Catholics, their bishops may serve as teachers of moral doctrine. There are, in addition, specific evils in society that Christian bishops should publicly condemn ("prophetically," if you will): racial oppression and anti-Semitism are clear candidates. But is it incumbent upon bishops of the church to get into the details of policy alternatives? Would it not be more useful if they were to raise incisive moral questions and put them to *all* partisans? The Simon/Novak document represents a clear example of Catholics coming out on one side of a particular set of issues. Others have come out on the other side. In a society increasingly polarized by political and ideological issues, bishops and other religious spokesmen are in a unique position to mediate, to challenge, to civilize. But as in labor/management relations, one cannot be a mediator and a partisan at the same time.

Archbishop Weakland and others remind us that the pastoral letter is only a first draft, and there is a year remaining for second thoughts. Given the dynamics of this sort of process, one cannot be hopeful that the document adopted by the full assembly of bishops will differ significantly from this draft, or will reverse its basic thrust. Thus, at the end of the year the bishops of the Catholic Church in America will have taken another major step toward a fairly narrow political partisanship. Since many of their people are evidently moving in a different political direction, this will create practical problems for the bishops (as it has for Methodist bishops). For many Catholics it may also occasion serious anguish.

As for the rest of us, if the bishops were simply engaged here in an academic exercise, we could say that they are not doing a very impressive job of it and be done. Their claim, however, is much more ambitious. They insist that they are engaged in a morally informed understanding, indeed, that they are exercising a "prophetic mandate" based on the "preferential option for the poor." In the end, therefore, a moral judgment of their performance is also called for.

No one can be sure what the outcome of any sound policy will be, but there is good reason to believe that the strategy to which the bishops are committing the prestige of the church may end by harming rather than helping the poor. Human lives are at stake: by what right, then, do these men appear before us, wrapped in the mantle of authority of prophets and popes stretching back to ancient Israel, and dare to tell us that one set of highly precarious policy choices represents the will of God in our time?

The Lessons of Europe

ROBERT J. SAMUELSON

THE BISHOPS WHO DRAFTED the recent pastoral letter on the American economy could usefully spend a few weeks touring Europe. They might learn there what they obviously did not learn here: social conscience is not enough; it won't produce economic justice. The principles the bishops admire most are enshrined in Europe and, partially as a result, Europe's economy is mired in massive unemployment.

The contrast with the United States could not be more vivid. Since 1974, Europe's economy hasn't created a single new job. The unemployment rate for non-Communist Europe is now hovering around 11 per cent, up from 3.1 per cent in 1974. Over the same period, the American economy has generated nearly 19 million new jobs; unemployment has risen, from 5.5 per cent in 1974 to 7.4 per cent in October 1984, but the increase has hardly matched the tripling of Europe's jobless rate.

What the bishops want is what Europe has striven to achieve: a humane capitalism. The bishops ask that every economic decision be judged (as their press release puts it) "primarily by the effect it will have on human beings." This insistence that ethical considerations dominate economic decisions is dangerous precisely because it seems so reasonable. In Europe, the practical consequences of this mentality—a highly generous welfare system and elaborate protection of workers' rights—perversely act to stymie job creation.

This apparent paradox is what makes the bishops' letter troubling. It is an exercise in economic make-believe. I am not saying that the morality of capitalism is above reproach. Most of us do not see the economy as an end in itself but as a means to other desirable ends—greater prosperity, less suffering, more freedom. We generally believe that the acts of governments, businesses, and labor unions ought to pass a higher standard of public good. But

Robert J. Samuelson is a columnist for *Newsweek*. This article is reprinted by permission from the December 3, 1984, issue of that magazine (© 1984 by Newsweek, Inc.; all rights reserved).

that said, and the bishops notwithstanding, most of our economic decisions can't be made as a matter of morality.

The economy's essential driving forces remain self-interest and specialization as identified by Adam Smith. You may call this greed, but it's really something else. Most of us lack the information to make decisions on ethical grounds, even if we wanted to. Consider a corporate purchasing agent who must buy either American-made steel at $500 a ton or foreign steel at $450. Is he choosing between American and foreign steel workers? Who is *morally* most deserving? If he buys the more expensive steel, is he weakening his own firm and jeopardizing its workers? He cannot easily predict the economic consequences of his decision, let alone its moral correctness.

Moral Superiority of Capitalism

All economies—capitalist, Communist, and those in between—inevitably consist of billions of daily bargains being made on the basis of self-interest and limited information. The moral superiority of capitalism is that it provides the best signals for maximizing production and, thereby, limiting human want. This genius, though, is also its Achilles' heel because it is given to fits of instability and judges people only on the basis of their economic usefulness. The modern welfare state is our compromise attempt to keep capitalism compassionate.

But it is a compromise, and the bishops seem unwilling or incapable of recognizing this. Efforts to make the economic system more "fair" may backfire by perversely changing the self-interest of businesses, workers, and other private decision-makers. Europe's inability to create jobs is a good example. In effect, hiring new workers has become too expensive. Wages are too high, payroll taxes (which, to firms, are another cost of labor) to finance welfare programs are too high, and profits have been too low. Once hired, workers can't easily be fired. European companies have reacted to these pressures by devoting more of their investment to substituting machines for people. If hiring is made unprofitable, firms don't hire.

No one intended this. Surely the unions that worked to raise their members' living standards and guarantee their jobs did not. Nor did the governments that acted to assure a decent living to those who could not work. (In Germany, unemployment insurance for workers with average wages is about 67 per cent of their normal pay; in the United States, it is about 36 per cent.)

Still, the result is a debilitating paralysis: high wages and welfare hamper job creation, yet welfare cannot easily be cut precisely when it seems most needed.

Creating a Socially Just Economy

I am not saying that this is the only reason for Europe's unemployment (American interest rates have probably contributed) or that all efforts to improve capitalism's social consequences are doomed to failure. But the insights of Adam Smith have not endured for two centuries because he had a good literary agent. A socially just economy is not primarily a matter of charity or good intentions. It is a matter of creating social policies that suppress the worst features of totally unfettered markets without destroying the inherent rewards and disciplines of a properly functioning market economy.

Because the bishops ignore these ambiguities, they have produced a document that is often irrelevant or, worse, immoral on its own terms. Everyone would like to reduce unemployment to 3 or 4 per cent, as the bishops urge. But suppose such a policy produces inflationary expectations—as it did in the 1960s and 1970s—and then inflation and, finally, an anti-inflationary reaction that causes higher unemployment. Can the policy be seen as relevant or moral?

There may be better ways to reconcile economic justice with economic efficiency. But the bishops have not helped us grope toward a superior system. The adverse reaction to their letter is not a measure of society's selfishness but a gut feeling that the moral problems of modern capitalism are more difficult than they seemed twenty years ago or than the bishops now think. No one says that balancing the impersonal pressures of markets against the desire to humanize capitalism is easy. But the bishops hardly tried. They seem to believe that the main problem is greed—that being more generous, we could do better. Having assumed that the problem is greed, they attempted to swamp us in guilt. It is the wrong response to the wrong problem.

God's Liberal Agenda

George F. Will

THE NATIONAL CONFERENCE OF CATHOLIC BISHOPS has discovered that God subscribes to the liberal agenda. But, then, in the mental world to which the bishops, in their flight from complexity, have immigrated, there are no intellectual difficulties, no insoluble problems. There are only shortages of good will.

With an almost—but not quite—comic sense of moral bravery and intellectual orginality, they hurl clichés at problems that have proven intractable in the face of strenuous efforts by persons of intelligence and dedication. The bishops thereby convict themselves of, at best, child-like innocence, or (this is a small step from innocence in adults) vanity.

All the important social-policy discussions of the last decade evidently occurred without the bishops' noticing. There have been sobering experiences concerning the complex and often deleterious effects of foreign aid. But the bishops just say: more, and better.

We now know a lot about how little we know about how to break the cycle of welfare dependency, or long-term employment. But the bishops, ignoring the principle that "ought" implies "can," simply postulate a duty to cleanse this sad old world of blemishes. Third World debt? The bishops say: Lighten the burden. And so on, and on, and on.

At one point the text says that "some" inequality may be acceptable, even desirable. However, in the introductory outline the bishops say: "There is a strong presumption against inequality of income or wealth as long as there are poor, hungry, and homeless people in our midst." So: there is a strong presumption against even the best societies the world has known, as long as they have the defects common to every society the world has known.

George F. Will is a nationally syndicated columnist and political analyst. This article is reprinted by permission of the Washington Post Writers' Group.

Some of the extremism in the proposed pastoral letter may just reflect the sort of sloppy writing that reflects the minds of persons who, marinated in a conventional wisdom, confuse exhortation with argument. The bishops say that the distribution of income in America is so inequitable that "it violates the minimum standard of distributive justice." Note well: the "minimum" standard. This is the bishops' idea of pastoral guidance—telling the most successful society the world has known that it is beneath even minimal standards.

The bishops have caught the disease that has ruined the "peace movement." It is the disease of moral complacency, born of sloth. The bishops attempt to achieve moral ascendancy by endorsing, with an air of heroism, an unexceptionable goal (for example, full employment or the elimination of poverty) while ignoring the fact that the serious argument is about means.

American capitalism is the most efficient antipoverty machine the world has seen. It is arguable that, at this point, less government action would serve the poor by enhancing the general growth of the economy. That may be mistaken, but is not self-evidently so. The bishops are unconvincing because they have an air of never entertaining a doubt about government programs, the effectiveness of which are now questioned by liberals as well as conservatives.

While offering perfunctory disapproval of statism, the bishops propose an enormous expansion of the power of the state as an allocator of wealth and enforcer of equality of conditions. The Conference of Bishops is located in Washington. Small wonder it has come to sound like just another liberal lobby. A few more such political platforms and the bishops will have reduced themselves to just another reedy voice in the capital's chorus, part of Washington's audible wallpaper: always there, never noticed.

What now will issue from the conference—the correct Christian position on soybean subsidies? Well, why not, now that the bishops have seen fit to invest more of their finite and wasting moral capital in putting God on the side of a liberal agenda, from jobs programs and increased day-care facilities through "global affirmative action."

As was the case last year when the subject was nuclear strategy, the bishops share the opinions of most liberal institutions, incuding many in journalism, which faithfully (so to speak) amplify the bishops' political proclamations. Of course, on one subject the bishops and those institutions still, for the moment, disagree: abortion. (Those institutions will not change; I am not so sure about the bishops.) On abortion liberal opinion says: It is sinful (so to speak) to use religious doctrine to dictate public policy.

Many liberals claim to see a threat to "the American way"—even the seeds of theocracy—in the idea that obedience to God requires opposition to abortion. Will those people now deplore the bishops' ideal that Christianity, properly understood, requires comprehensive support for the standard liberal wish-list? No.

Squandering Moral Capital

PHILIP F. LAWLER

CITING THEIR DESIRE to avoid partisan politics, the American Catholic bishops waited until after the 1984 elections to release the first draft of their pastoral letter on economics. That restraint is admirable, but curious. If their letter asserts Roman Catholic doctrine, why should the bishops worry about its political impact? Suppose the Albigensian heresy cropped up again in the middle of an election year; would the bishops wait until the polls closed before defending Catholic dogma?

On the other hand, if the pastoral letter goes beyond the scope of Catholic teaching, why are the bishops venturing so far afield? The Catholic tradition involves a clear division of labor: Bishops are to proclaim general moral principles; the political chore of enacting those principles falls to Catholic laymen. So when the bishops endorse specific public policies, they are trespassing on the layman's territory.

Unfortunately, the American bishops have been trespassing more and more blatantly in recent years, and they have enjoyed the experience. Father J. Bryan Hehir—the chief architect of last year's pastoral letter on nuclear weaponry, and the resident political guru of the bishops' staff—delights in telling audiences that the bishops' political activity is hard to classify: they side with the new right on abortion, with the new left on defense and economic strategy. But a political maverick is not necessarily a political innocent, and anyone who doubts the bishops' political ambitions need only consult their latest product.

The pastoral letter on nuclear weapons came as a shock to an unprepared Catholic laity. Not so this effort. Informed Catholics have been expecting the bishops' economic statement for months, and a group chaired by William Simon and Michael Novak managed to beat the bishops to press with a pastoral letter of their own. For months, the bishops and their staff have known that their statement would face vocal and organized criticism. Even before the two documents were released, interesting skirmishes had occurred.

Philip F. Lawler is president of the American Catholic Conference, a lay Catholic group located in Washington, D.C. This article is reprinted from the *Wall Street Journal*, November 13, 1984 (© 1984, The Dow Jones Company).

Early in the drafting process, the bishops seemed to relish the idea of another heated controversy. Months ago, the dean of the bishops' staff (Monsignor George Higgins) predicted that the economic statement would be "far more controversial than the peace pastoral." Bishop J. Francis Stafford of Memphis came to New York to denounce the Lay Commission on Catholic Social Teaching and the U.S. Economy. At a meeting of the Catholic Press Association, Archbishop Rembert G. Weakland of Milwaukee, chairman of the bishops' drafting committee, urged Catholic newspaper editors to censor columns and ignore letters from Lay Commission supporters. Then gradually the controversy cooled down. Archbishop Weakland met with Messrs. Simon and Novak and, at least publicly, welcomed their interest. And Monsignor Higgins told *Business Week* that "Michael Novak is going to have a hard time finding anything that he basically disagrees with" in the document.

Actually, Mr. Novak might find something to disagree with on virtually every one of the document's 112 pages. The bishops' draft provides a barrage of highly specific economic proposals and conclusions: endorsing the New International Economic Order; condemning flat-tax proposals; demanding increased U.S. contributions to the soft-loan window of the World Bank; and asserting that the maximum allowable unemployment rate is between 3 per cent and 4 per cent. True, the draft admits that men of good will might disagree with some of those proposals. But it also questions the virtue of anyone who argues that there is a connection between culture and poverty, or claims that the private sector generates employment more efficiently than the government.

Why do the bishops put their moral authority behind such highly controversial propositions? It is possible that they are not acquainted with the competing ideas. Despite repeated protests from concerned laymen—again led by Mr. Novak—the bishops' drafting committee recruited a staff monopolized by the political left. The draft document cites a host of liberal economists, ignoring any work by more conservative scholars.

The Key Weakness

The key weakness of the bishops' analysis comes at the outset. In the second sentence of their draft, the bishops announce: "Every perspective on economic life that is human, moral, and Christian must be shaped by two questions: What does it do *for* people? What does it do *to* people?" Nowhere do the bishops discuss what people might do to, for, or through the economic system. No, the system is seen as some monolithic force, acting upon people rather than being shaped by their actions.

As a practical matter, that anthropomorphic attitude toward the economic "system" translates into an emphasis on the role of government. In fact, the bishops seem to believe that the government controls and directs the economy; hence their emphasis on governmental solutions to every economic woe. Are the bishops doomed to promote government involvement even when (as happens too often in the Third World) government involvment is already stifling the chances of development?

By concentrating on the government, the bishops underestimate the moral importance of the individual as an economic actor. The draft document virtually dismisses the possibility of individual charity as a solution to poverty. And the letter thoroughly goes against the traditional Catholic doctrine of "subsidiarity," which demands that, whenever possible, economic and social authority should be vested in individuals rather than in communities.

Both the bishops and their lay counterparts frequently allude to the Pope's persistent criticisms of Western economies. But both the bishops and the Lay Commission miss the point of John Paul II's critique. As the Pope frequently has stressed, he objects primarily to the impact of excessive materialism in the West. Materialism is a moral disorder that afflicts individuals, and can be corrected only by pointing those individuals toward higher moral precepts. After all, it is individuals—not economic systems—that face heaven or hell; so it is the business of the church to save individual souls. In days past, bishops devoted most of their energies to that effort.

Effect on Laymen Who Differ

When they endorse particular economic plans in such excruciating detail, the bishops necessarily place themselves in opposition to many devout Catholics who favor different approaches. (During the 1984 campaign, when they spoke out on abortion, the bishops offered no such detailed remedies, only a general moral principle. In the past, however, they have endorsed a particular anti-abortion measure; in that case, too, they overstepped their bounds.)

If the debate over the "peace pastoral" provides any guidance, the bishops will give scant attention to the possibility that some laymen share their goals—in this case, serving the needs of the poor—but distrust the particular solutions the bishops have proposed. To some bishops, and to many of the staff aides who prepare and promote these documents, political opposition merely confirms that they are on the right track.

As with the peace pastoral, the bishops will receive plenty of congratulations for their work on economics. But the congratulations will come disproportionately from the secular media, from academe, and from liberal political activists. It's an echo chamber, really, because those are precisely the groups whose lead the bishops have been following. We shall hear a good deal about the "prophetic" nature of the bishops' work from people who ordinarily do not believe in prophecy. No one should fault the bishops for attempting to influence secular culture, but one can certainly ask who is influencing whom.

Meanwhile, back in the pews, the ordinary lay Catholic might be wondering why the bishops are so heavily involved in public policy, when their church has so many troubles of its own. Few laymen will read the bishops' final product, especially if additions and amendments expand it beyond its present 112-page length; they too will receive their information from the newspaper accounts. Traditionally, a pastoral letter is read aloud to the Catholic faithful at Sunday Mass. The new brand of political pastorals aims for an entirely different audience.

But for the Catholic Church, that is only a secondary problem. Today, one group of Catholics, having rejected church teachings on matters such as birth control, listens to the bishops only when the topic is political. Another group, loyal to the hierarchy on doctrinal issues, grows increasingly frustrated by the bishops' involvement in public policy. As Catholic laymen grow accustomed to following their bishops selectively, the time may be coming— it may already be here—when the bishops lose their ability to sway their flocks even on questions that do involve fundamental Catholic dogma. Forgive me, fathers, but aren't you squandering your moral capital?

Catholic Social Teaching and the Limits of Authority

John J. O'Connor

SOME OBSERVERS HAVE SUGGESTED that the bishops' discussion of economic concerns will somehow put them in a new and different role. It is important to correct that misperception. There is, in fact, a long tradition of Catholic teaching on economic matters. The upcoming pastoral letter will take its place in this ongoing tradition of social teaching—a teaching that has its roots in Abraham, Moses, the prophets, and in the very life and message of Jesus himself.

Catholic social teaching of the past 100 years includes a body of documents that have provided a systematic and normative theory relating the social vision of our faith to concrete conditions of the modern world. Each of the documents that constitute this body of Catholic teaching was, in its own way, a response to the "signs of the times." Each attempted to offer serious moral teaching and reflection on major questions of the day. Without attempting a comprehensive overview of these documents, I would like to highlight several of the major elements and stages of development that make up this important part of our religious tradition.

Catholic social teaching in the latter nineteenth century and early twentieth century focuses primarily on questions of economic justice in the context of the Industrial Revolution. For example, in the encyclical *Rerum Novarum*

John J. O'Connor, Archbishop of New York, oversees the department of international justice and peace at the U.S. Catholic Conference. Formerly bishop of the Catholic Military Ordinariate, he was a member of the drafting committee for the bishops' pastoral letter on war and peace. This is a slightly abridged version of the 1984 Labor Day Message of the Conference, written before—but with an eye toward—the publication of the bishops' letter on the economy. It is reprinted by permission of the U.S. Catholic Conference and the Archdiocese of New York.

in 1891, Pope Leo XIII strongly defended the rights of workers and argued for more humane working conditions. He criticized the excessive concentration of wealth, defended the right to private property, and called on the state to serve the common good.

In 1931 Pope Pius XI's encyclical *Quadragesimo Anno* reiterated and renewed some of the same themes—criticizing economic greed and the excessive concentration of ownership, defending the right of workers to collective bargaining, and calling for just wages and a more equitable distribution of created goods.

The outbreak of World War II, followed by post-war political, economic, and social developments, introduced a new set of issues which required analysis from the perspective of the church's teaching. One of the new "signs of the times" was the growing interdependence of nations and economies throughout the world. This theme becomes very prominent in church documents of the post-war period.

Pope John XXIII's encyclical *Mater et Magistra* in 1961 reflected on technical and scientific progress and on the heightened complexity and interdependence of social and economic relations around the world. The Holy Father spoke strongly about the basic rights of the poor and the positive role of government in promoting the common good. Pope John also asserted that working men and women should acquire some share in productive enterprises and should have an ample portion of the fruits of production. In commenting on the economy as a whole, the Holy Father wrote that "the economic prosperity of any people is to be assessed not so much from the sum total of goods and wealth possessed as from the distribution of goods according to the norms of justice."

Pope John XXIII's last encyclical, *Pacem in Terris,* was issued in 1963. In it he further developed the church's teaching on basic human rights and obligations, and he did so in a context that strongly emphasized the social nature of human beings and the paramount goal of working for the common good.

Pope Paul VI's *Populorum Progressio* (1967) took the teaching on economic justice another step forward. In it the pope reminded the affluent of their duties to the poor. He again emphasized the international aspects of social and economic justice by addressing such topics as development assistance to poor nations and improving trade relations.

A new stage of development in Catholic social teaching was marked by Pope Paul VI's 1971 apostolic letter *Octogesima Adveniens.* This letter addressed the "new social questions of post-industrial society." It recapitulated major themes from earlier documents but opened up new issues for discussions as well. The "new social questions" which Paul VI identified are those that arise from societies that have gone through the Industrial Revolution and are now highly urbanized, pluralistic, and secular—societies that are greatly influenced by mass communications and continually changed by technological innovations.

In our time, the encyclicals of Pope John Paul II have been dramatic examples of reading the signs of the times and reflecting on them from the perspective of Catholic social thought. His most recent encyclical, *Laborem Exercens,* is particularly relevant in that it serves to sum up much of the earlier social teaching and to advance it very significantly in several areas. Using the central theme of the dignity of human work, Pope John Paul addresses a wide range of issues that are crucial to the daily lives of working men and women around the world. He speaks of the importance of work in human society and the corresponding evils of unemployment. He speaks of just wages, the importance of unions, the need for workers to become owners of the means of production, and the positive responsibility of government to ensure jobs for those who can work and adequate income for those who cannot.

Previous Bishops' Statements

Church teaching on economic issues has not been limited to papal and synodal documents from Rome. The Catholic bishops in the United States and in other nations have periodically issued documents of their own which serve to apply the universal teaching of the church to the more specific and sometimes unique circumstances of their own countries: As Pope Paul VI said in *Octogesima Adveniens:* "It is up to the Christian communities to analyze with objectivity the situation which is proper to their own country, to shed on it the light of the Gospel's unalterable words and to draw principles of reflection, norms of judgment and directives for action from the social teaching of the church."

This is precisely what the bishops have in mind in developing a pastoral letter on the U.S. economy. While the pastoral letter is expected to be a document of major significance, it is by no means the first time the U.S. bishops will have spoken on economic issues in this country. Indeed, what may be called the Magna Carta of social action for the American church was the

"Bishops' Program of Social Reconstruction" issued in 1919 by the National Catholic War Council, which was the forerunner of the U.S. Catholic Conference. This remarkable statement, prepared for the bishops by Msgr. John A. Ryan, included a list of far-sighted and far-reaching recommendations for reforms in economic policy. For example, the statement called for minimum-wage legislation, government regulation of public-service monopolies, growth of industrial co-operatives, equal pay for women, just wages, public housing and insurance programs, and the right of labor to organize and bargain collectively.

Since 1919 the U.S. bishops' conference has continued to issue statements in response to changing economic and social conditions in society. For example, in 1930 the bishops' administrative board issued a statement on unemployment in which they said:

> This unemployment returning again to plague us after so many repetitions during the century past is a sign of deep failure in our country. Unemployment is the great peacetime physical tragedy of the nineteenth and twentieth centuries, and both in its cause and in the imprint it leaves upon those who inflict it, those who permit it and those who are its victims, it is one of the great moral tragedies of our time.

In 1975 the U.S. bishops issued "The Economy: Human Dimensions." This document recalled some of the major ethical norms of Catholic social teaching and addressed a series of current problems including unemployment, inflation, and the maldistribution of income and wealth in the American economy. The statement declared that "full employment is the foundation of a just economic policy and should not be sacrificed for other political and economic goals." The statement called for better co-operation between the private and public sectors of the economy, for fairness in taxation, and for a more responsible stewardship of the land in our nation.

Even this very brief review of a small selection of Catholic statements on economic issues serves to illustrate, in my judgment, the consistency with which the church has expressed its concern for economic justice in different times and in different social and economic settings. To undertake the development of a pastoral letter on economic issues in our time and in our nation is not, therefore, a sudden shift in church practices; nor is it merely a response to popular pressures or trends. It is rather a continuation of a long and important tradition in the church.

As the church prepares to open discussion of the forthcoming pastoral letter on economics, it is important to reflect on the fact that we are not only a community of believers but a major social institution in a pluralistic society. As a "public church" we believe that we have not only the right but also the responsibility to contribute to public debate on major issues of our day.

The pastoral letter on war and peace was an important development in the church's growing awareness of its role as a public actor in the wider life of society and of how it may carry out this role appropriately and competently. The pastoral letter was successful in helping to open public debate to moral analysis of issues relating to war and peace. In a similar way, the pastoral letter on the economy will attempt to help open public debate to more explicit moral analysis of economic issues. In doing so, the church is not "intruding" in political affairs or adding an alien issue to the public debate. Rather it is seeking to make clear the human and moral consequences of the technical choices we make as a nation.

Critical Economic Choices

The headlines of the daily newspapers provide ample evidence of the critical economic choices that face our nation at this point in history. Changes in the world economy and in our own economy have raised new problems and new challenges. These are not purely academic or technical issues to be left in the hands of a small group of experts. Rather, they are public issues that affect the lives and fortunes of virtually every citizen of this nation. It is deeply important, therefore, that we do our part to ensure that these crucial issues are decided, not only on the basis of "hard facts" and scientific calculations, but also on the basis of fundamental human values, moral wisdom, and religious inspiration.

To engage in this kind of moral reflection on economic issues is neither simple nor easy. It involves affirming the great successes of the American economy as well as raising—without regard to any party or particular administration—serious and challenging questions about some of our practices and policies as a nation on both the individual and institutional levels. It is important that we do not allow these complexities and fears to paralyze our ability to engage in serious moral reflection and judgment on economic matters. Such reflection is, on the one hand, beneficial and necessary for the church, for it is carrying out the gospel mandate to re-evaluate every aspect of our lives in the light of Jesus' life and teaching. On the other hand, it is beneficial and necessary for society because it is an affirmation of our democratic political heritage and institutions. It is a sign of our dedication to democracy when we strive to make a genuine and unique contribution to public discourse on these vital issues.

When the bishops as moral teachers attempt to engage the church and the broader society in moral reflection on complex social issues, they do so with a style of teaching that includes different levels of moral authority. As we said in the pastoral letter on peace:

> We do not intend that our treatment of each of these issues carry the same moral authority as our statement of universal moral principles and formal church teaching. Indeed, we stress here at the beginning that not every statement in this letter has the same moral authority. At times we reassert universally binding moral principles. . . . At other times we reaffirm statements of recent popes and the teaching of Vatican II. Again, at other times we apply moral principles to specific cases. When making applications of these principles we realize . . . that prudential judgments are involved based on specific circumstances which can change or which can be interpreted differently by people of good will.